The Art *of* Pickleball

Techniques and Strategies for Everyone

Gale H. Leach

Acacia Publishing
Phoenix, Arizona

The Art of Pickleball:
Techniques and Strategies
for Everyone

Published by Acacia Publishing
1366 E. Thomas, Suite 305
Phoenix, AZ 85014
www.acaciapublishing.com

Second Edition
Copyright © 2008 by Gale H. Leach
Printed in the United States of America

Illustrations by Gale Leach and Travis Leach
Photographs by Richard Leach, Gale Leach, Morgan Engel, Matt Derry
Book and cover design by Gale Leach

International Standard Book Number:
    ISBN-13: 978-0-9814629-8-1
    ISBN-10: 0-9814629-8-7

Acknowledgements

Many people helped with the creation of this book. I would like to thank:

... my husband, Richard, who provided inspiration, encouragement, laughter, proofreading, and help with photos. Besides being my life partner, he's also a fun pickleball partner.

... my son, Travis, for giving life to the little people who romp through the illustrations on these pages.

... my son, Morgan, and my almost son, Matt Derry, for taking great pictures.

... Millie Amburgy, Vic and Pauline Avery, Bill Booth, Claude Eatherly, Sue Gardiner, Pat Kane, Pete Kendall, John and Doisey Landry, Jim Lewis, and Denise and Dick Williams who reviewed the text and graphics and helped make this book much better.

... Vic and Pauline Avery, Rock Kane, Matt Derry, Morgan Engel, Candace Brostrum and others at Sun City Grand for letting me videotape their play and posing for photographs.

... the Sun City Grand Pickleball Club for providing the opportunity to learn and love the sport of pickleball, and for Bill Booth's tips on their web site that started the seed for this book.

... our cats, Rigel, Orion, and Bella for help with "keyboarding" and making sure I took play breaks.

... and the readers (you) who bought this book and are enjoying playing pickleball.

Thank you all,

Gale Leach
www.galeleach.com/pickleball/

People Who Helped with This Book

The following people provided information, reviewed content, and offered suggestions, all of which helped make this book become a reality. This is not a comprehensive list. I wish I could thank everyone who helped—some of you didn't even realize you were helping—and if I've forgotten anyone, I hope you will forgive me.

In 2002, Bill Booth founded the pickleball club at Sun City Grand in Surprise, AZ, and has promoted the sport by giving introductory lessons to well over 500 prospective players. He also maintains the web site for the United States of America Pickleball Association (http://www.usapa.org). He's won a scattering of medals over the years but feels that's not the most important thing. "The top players are not necessarily the best teachers, and sometimes the best teachers are not great players. The best teachers have studied the game and can express it well. Some of the top players know the strategy instinctively, but would have trouble expressing it. I guess that I am a little of each."

Sue Gardiner taught high school physical education for 29 years and coached high school girls tennis for 10 years. She was Southern California CIF Coach of the Year for Tennis in 1985 and Teacher of the Year in 1990. Sue has been playing pickleball for about seven years and has won numerous medals in various competitions since 2004. Sue is consistently one of the best players in the game.

Denise Williams is a past President of the Sun City Grand Pickleball Club and is active in competition throughout the Phoenix, AZ, area. Denise has played pickleball for about nine years. She is a very strong competitor and enjoys instructing others in playing the game. Denise has also taken her share of medals at various local tournaments.

Dick Williams served 33 years in law enforcement until he retired in 1995 as the elected Sheriff of San Bernardino County, California. During his career, Dick served as training academy director and physical education instructor. He found pickleball as he traveled across the country as a member of the Thousand Trails camping system. After seven years of play, Dick is a top competitor and instructor and won a bronze medal in the Utah Senior Olympic Games.

Pauline Avery learned how to play tennis late in life and couldn't get enough of it, sometimes playing twice a day. She joined a tennis club and played a lot of women's doubles with her partner, and they won many trophies through the years.

After Pauline and Vic married, they played competitive doubles tennis as partners and did well. Two years ago, however, they found it harder and harder to find tennis couples to pair with, so they moved to Sun City Grand. When they got there, however, they got hooked on playing pickleball. They have all but given up tennis for this engaging sport. Pauline played in her first pickleball tournament in Mesa, AZ, and she and her partner won a bronze medal. A year later, she won two gold medals at the Sun City Grand Tournament, and she has continued to add medals to her collection nearly everywhere she plays.

Vic Avery is also a former tennis player, although he plays rarely now. Along with Pauline, Vic discovered pickleball about two years ago and now plays regularly. He says that tennis matches are still difficult to arrange, but "I can walk onto the pickleball courts any morning and find comparable players. Also, pickleball players are not as stuffy as tennis players as a rule." He also helps in instructing beginning and improving pickleball players on a regular basis. Vic has played in quite a few tournaments and has won nearly as many medals, some with Pauline. Vic says he will never be a great player, but he loves the game, as do most who try it.

Claude and Sherry Eatherly first played pickleball in 2003. Being competitive, Claude sought to play with the more highly skilled players and improved his skill level quickly. Sherry chose to improve her skills playing with the C- & B-level drop-in groups. Claude won a silver medal at his first tournament in April 2004 and soon after placed third in his division in the Arizona Senior Olympics. Since then, he has played in quite a few other tournaments. At a later, local tournament, Claude was paired with Ann Almoney, a C-level player, and they took the gold in their flight—quite an accomplishment for Ann, a relatively new player. Sherry also won a silver medal at a local tournament in March 2005. Both Claude and Sherry are certified referees and enjoy teaching new and mid-level players.

John Landry has played tennis since high school and is currently on the A ladder at Sun City Grand. Doisey Landry played tennis most of her adult life and currently plays on the novice ladder. They say they are very much surprised how pickleball has taken over tennis in their lives. "We tried this unheard of sport to humor friends a year ago, when first moving to Sun City Grand. We have not been on the tennis court since. We aspire to play this game into our 'old age.'"

Pat Kane started playing pickleball in the Seattle area around 1987. He relayed an interesting story: "My partner and I were both hard hitters, and we thought we were good players until we entered a tournament and played against two women who knew how to dink the ball and slow it down. Needless to say, we lost to these two women—what a blow—and I vowed that would never happen again. From then on I became a finesse player instead of hitting the ball hard all the time. My advice to anyone who wants to become good is to learn the slow game and, of course, get a good partner who plays the same way that you do."

for Richard
who makes my heart smile

for Travis, Scott, and Morgan
who are the lights of my life

and for my Mom
who taught me to be self-reliant
and gave me courage

A Note about Pronouns

English does not yet have a personal pronoun that is understood as either gender. I once tried using "s/he" in my writing, but it wasn't well received. In this book, I use the male pronouns "he," "him," and "his," not in preference for men (although I like them), but because I believe women are generally more tolerant of such things. Women, thanks for your understanding.

Contents

Figures

Introduction

Pickleball is a fun, fast-paced game that is gaining popularity around the world. It is easy to learn, can be played well by people of all ages in a relatively short period of time, and the small size of the court allows it to be played nearly anywhere.

When I was learning to play pickleball, I looked for books that would explain how to become a better player. Because the sport was still relatively new, only a couple of books were available. Not finding exactly what I was looking for, I decided to write it.

This book is the culmination of interviews with many players, both novice and veteran, examination of what excellent players do that novice players do not, research through books, videos, and online sources, and my notes as I learned the sport and became a better player.

Few of you will read this book from cover to cover. Books of this sort usually have too much information in them for that kind of reading to be useful. Only the information that you're ready for—that takes you from where you are today to a step above that—will make sense and really be useful.

If you do read all of the material here, you'll find some conflicting information. Not all of the people I interviewed agree on the best way to make a shot or when you should take certain actions. I have included the different methods when there was significant disagreement or when I felt multiple options might help you discover what would work best for you. As in any sport, there seem to be many "right" ways to do things that are all different from one another. In this book, I've tried to present what seems to be the right way, when possible, based on a agreement among my sources. Where differences were significant, I've made that clear and presented both sides. It's up to you do decide what you like.

I hope you will read the sections of this book that interest you now and browse the rest from time to time. Perhaps you'll leave this book sitting out on your coffee table and pick it up periodically. Books like this can be read and read again as your skills improve and you learn more about the game. Perhaps later you'll discover new things upon rereading a passage that you missed the first time, or you'll find new interest in something you weren't ready for earlier.

That's the best reason to come back and read this book: as your game improves, you will need to change your techniques and strategies, and you'll be seeking new information. Here's a general plan for learning and improving your pickleball game.

- **Learn how to play and practice.** New players should read all the rules and learn the basics of how to hit the ball and move on the court. Then study new ways to hone your skills as you improve. You can learn by watching and talking with players who are better than you, analyzing what they're doing and why, and playing games with them. Have someone videotape your play and watch it to see what you're really doing, not what you think you do. Make sure you're doing it right from the beginning so you don't have to unlearn things later. Once you've addressed any bad habits and replaced them with good ones, you'll see your game improve rapidly.

- **Learn to warm up and stretch properly, and do it *every* time you play.** Pickleball is easy to pick up quickly, but that doesn't mean you shouldn't treat it as seriously as any other sport. Unhappily, injuries in pickleball are common and fall into two main categories: not warming up enough before play and going past your limits during play. Only you know your limits, and occasionally you may find yourself going after a ball that is beyond your reach. Warming up properly is something you *can* do, however, and I encourage you not to overlook ensuring that your body is as ready to play as you are.

- **Practice the skills you know and learn new ones.** There it is: you won't get better without practice. Pickleball practice should be fun and easy. Pickleball is such a great sport that people enjoy going out to practice sometimes more than they like playing competitive games. Remember—you can learn from mistakes as well as from the greatest shots. Go out and play!

- **Become a better partner.** Having good communication on the court is primary, but there are other ways to play better together, too. Finding out what these are can make doubles play even more enjoyable and allow you to win more often. Talk with your partner about things you can do to improve your communication and rhythm on the court, as well as how to minimize your weaknesses and maximize your strengths.

- **Have fun.** Pickleball is gaining popularity because it's easy to learn and fun to play. In your zeal to become a better player, don't become frustrated or angry if you have a bad day or lose a match. Remember, like any other endeavor, you will become better with practice, and you'll always play better if you relax. Be kind to yourself. Enjoy the game and have fun.

I've included a glossary of terms in this introductory material and the complete rules in an appendix. Check my web site for resources for pickleball equipment and information.

If you are new to the sport, beware: pickleball is addictive. One friend told me he moved to an active adult community for the numerous golf courses located there. He then decided to try pickleball and found he enjoyed it more than golfing.

I hope you enjoy this book. I enjoyed writing it, and I learned a lot from the other players who shared their expertise and stories. I hope you'll contact me with comments, questions, or suggestions. I'd love to hear from you. Please send your comments to:

Gale H. Leach
pickleball@gmail.com   www.galeleach.com

A Short History of the Sport

One summer day in 1965, Bill Bell and Joel Pritchard (then a U.S. Congressman) returned to Pritchard's Seattle-area home to find their families together there, complaining that they were bored. The men began searching for the long-lost badminton equipment to go with the court on the Pritchard's property. They found some racquets, not in the best of shape, and a net, but no birdie. A whiffle ball would have to do. The kids seemed to like the game, but the racquets didn't perform well with the 3-inch ball, so they made some wooden paddles. These seemed to work well, and the volleying continued happily for the rest of the afternoon.

The next morning, they found that the kids and moms were still enjoying the game, but they had lowered the net to tennis height and discovered that the ball bounced well on the pavement. They established a rule that made only underhand serves legal, creating a more fair play between the adults and kids (no overhead smash serves allowed).

Time went by and everyone continued to enjoy the new sport. Other friends who came by were introduced to the game, and finally the men decided to write a set of rules. They began with the rules of badminton, changing them to deal with the alterations they'd made for the equipment and changes in net height. As in badminton, only one serve per person was given, although they allowed the server to put one foot over the line (to accommodate a large tree that made it impossible to stand with both feet behind the line).

They'd already realized that the player at the net had a distinct advantage, so they made their new game more fair by creating a zone in the area from the net to the badminton service court line within which a player could not stand and volley the ball. (This was eventually extended to seven feet from the net and was renamed the "non-volley zone," or, as it's affectionately known where I play, "the kitchen.")

They had a great game. The Pritchard's cocker spaniel, Pickles, liked it, too. He would hide in the bushes and, as soon as a ball came his way, he'd dash out, grab the ball, and run away. The game, which had been so far unnamed, became known as "Pickles' Ball."

More rules were added as time went by. In 1967, Pritchard built the first actual pickleball court in his back yard and, over the next few years, more courts were built around the Seattle area. Now, pickleball is played as a competitive sport in the Senior Olympics, and many communities around the United States are building courts to accommodate the growing demand from local citizens. Schools and colleges have added pickleball into their curricula. It is my understanding that the sport has also become popular in Japan, and may be played in other countries as well. Not bad for something that started as an afternoon diversion to conquer boredom.[1]

---

1. This description compiled from information found in *Pickle-Ball for Player and Teacher* by Joyce M. Curtis, *The Official Pickleball Handbook* by Mark Friedenberg, SportsKnowHow.com, and information told to me by other players. See the references on page 143 for a complete description of the sources listed above.

Glossary of Terms

Ace—A serve that is not returned by the opponent.

Approach Shot— A shot hit forehand or backhand while running up to the net.

Backcourt—The area of the court within a few feet of the baseline.

Backhand—A stroke hit on the side of the body opposite from the hand holding the paddle.

Backspin—Spin imparted to the ball by stroking it from high to low, causing it to spin in the direction opposite to its flight. Also called underspin, slice, or chop.

Backswing—Moving the paddle back from the ready position to prepare for a shot.

Baseline—The line at the back of the pickleball court (22 feet from the net).

Bounce It—A directive from your partner to let the ball bounce (because your partner thinks it will land out of bounds).

Carry—Hitting the ball in such as way that it is carried along on the face of the paddle during its forward motion.

Centerline—The line bisecting the service courts that extends from the non-volley zone line to the baseline.

Chop—The motion from high to low that puts backspin on the ball.

Closed Face—The top of the paddle face is angled downward about 30 degrees from vertical.

Crosscourt—The opponent's court diagonally opposite yours.

Dead Ball—The ball is ruled to be dead when a fault is declared.

Deep—Far into the court, near the baseline.

Dink—A soft, low shot, initiated from within or just behind the non-volley zone, that lands in the opponent's non-volley zone.

Double Bounce Rule—After a serve, each team must play their first shot off the bounce, after which the ball can be played off the bounce or volleyed.

Doubles—A game played with four people divided into two teams, each team having two players. Teams can be two men, two women, or a woman and a man (mixed doubles).

Down the Line—A shot hit near a sideline that travels close and parallel to the same line.

Drive—A low shot hit to the opponent's backcourt.

Drop Shot— soft shot, usually initiated from mid- to backcourt, that arcs just over the net and lands within the opponent's non-volley zone.

Drop Shot Volley—A soft volley shot that is designed to slow the speed of the ball and return it short, just behind the net.

Even Court—The right half of the court. It is called this because, in singles, your score will be even when you are serving from this side.

Face—The broad surface on the head of the paddle used to hit the ball.

Flat Face—The hitting surface of the paddle is kept parallel to the net.

Fault—An infringement of the rules that ends the rally.

Follow Through—A continuation of the motion of your swing that follows the direction you wish the ball to travel.

Foot Fault—Failure to keep at least one foot behind the baseline and touching the ground at the moment the paddle contacts the ball during a serve, or stepping on or into the non-volley zone while volleying a ball.

Forehand—A stroke hit on the same side of the body as the hand holding the paddle.

Game—Regulation games are played to 11 points (a team must win by two points). Some local games are played to 15 points.

Grip—How you hold the handle of the paddle, or the material that is wrapped around the handle.

Ground Stroke—A stroke made after the ball has bounced.

Half Volley— A ground stroke in which the paddle contacts the ball after it bounces but before it rises to its potential height. Usually hit just a few inches from the ground.

Head— The part of the paddle above the handle that is used to hit the ball.

Kitchen— An affectionate name for the non-volley zone.

Let Serve— A serve that touches the top of the net and lands in the proper service court (it is replayed without penalty).

Lob— A shot that sends the ball high overhead and deep, forcing the opponent back to the baseline.

Midcourt— The area between the non-volley zone and the backcourt.

Non-Volley Zone— A seven-foot area adjacent to the net within which you may not volley the ball. The non-volley zone usually includes all lines around it.

Odd Court— The left half of the court. It is called this because, in singles, your score will be odd when you are serving from this side.

Open Face— The top of the paddle face is angled upward about 30 degrees from vertical.

Overhead Shot— A shot made with the paddle over head height. Often synonymous with smash or slam, although it can refer to any shot made at that height, whether hard or soft.

Passing Shot— A shot that passes beyond the reach of the player and lands in bounds. Typically played against an opponent who is advancing on the non-volley zone or who is already there.

Poach— In doubles, to cross over into your partner's area to play a ball.

Punch— A short, quick shot, without significant backswing or follow through, usually during a volley.

Put Away— A ball hit such that the opponent cannot return it. A winning shot.

Rally— Hitting the ball back and forth between opponents.

Serve (Service)—An underhand lob or drive stroke used to put a ball into play at the beginning of a point.

Server Number—When playing doubles, either "1" or "2," depending on whether you are the first or second server for your side. This number is appended to the score when it is called.

Shadowing—Moving in tandem with your partner so that you stay about 10 feet from each other and avoid leaving open spaces on your half of the court.

Shot—The flight of the ball after it leaves the paddle.

Sideline—The line at the side of the court.

Singles—A game played with two people, one on each side.

Slice—Another name for backspin or underspin.

Smash or Slam— A hard, overhead shot.

Stroke—The action of hitting the ball.

Technical Foul—The referee may add one point to a player's score or a team's score when, in the referee's judgment, the opponent is being deliberately abusive.

Topspin—Spin applied to the ball by stroking it from low to high, causing it to rotate in the direction of its flight.

Volley—To hit the ball before it bounces.

Chapter 1

Rules and Equipment

The complete rules for pickleball are available in Appendix A of this book and also on the web site of the United States of America Pickleball Association (USAPA; http://www.usapa.org). The November 2007 rules revision (included in this book) changed some rules significantly, but some other, more minor, rules changes are still under discussion. Revision of the rules is a continuing process as the game evolves, so please check the USAPA web site where the most current rules are posted.

Below is a synopsis of the basic rules of pickleball, followed by some lesser-known rules (which may surprise you).

The Basic Rules

- **The Serve.** You must serve underhand: your arm must be moving in an upward arc and the paddle head must be below your wrist when it strikes the ball. The paddle must contact the ball below your waist before the ball bounces. Both feet must be behind the baseline, and at least one of your feet must be in contact with the ground when the paddle contacts the ball. You must also serve from within the confines of the serving court. These confines lie behind the serving court baseline and on or between imaginary lines extended from the court centerline and the sideline. The ball must land in the diagonal backcourt behind the opponent's non-volley zone line. Only one serve attempt is allowed (unless the ball touches the net and then lands in the proper service court—such a serve is replayed). At the start of a game, the team that serves first is allowed only one fault before service transfers to their opponents. After that, each team member serves before the opponents begin serving. In singles play, the first serve is always made from the right-hand court; in doubles play, the player in the right-hand court always starts service for the team.

- **Return of Service in Doubles Play.** Only the designated receiver may return the serve. If the other player touches (or is touched by) the ball first, it is a fault.

- **Double Bounce Rule.** Each team must play the first ball off the bounce. After the ball is served and has bounced once on each side, teams can either play the ball off the bounce or volley it.

- **Volley.** It is a fault if you volley the ball when one (or both) of your feet is in the non-volley zone or on its line. You may step or stand in the non-volley zone at any time, but, if your feet are in this zone, you must play the ball off the bounce. It is not a fault if your paddle moves in the air over the non-volley zone.

- **Faults.** Play continues until a fault occurs. The ball must bounce within bounds. You may not touch any part of the net with your body, paddle, or clothing, although it is not a fault to swing your paddle over the net. You must hit the ball before it bounces twice on your side of the court. The ball must not hit the roof, walls, or other objects that are not part of the court. (See the complete rules in Appendix A or online for a list of all possible faults.)

- **Scoring.** A team can score points only when serving. Tournament games are played to eleven points, and a team must win by two points. Some local games are played to 15 or 21 points. The score and server number should be announced before every serve.

The Lesser-Known Rules

- Pickleballs are hard and do not flatten upon impact. Consequently, evaluating whether a pickleball is in or out requires determining where the center of the ball was when it landed. (Note that this is different from the rules of tennis, where balls tend to flatten out when they hit the playing surface, and so are ruled "in" if any part of a tennis ball hits the line.) As shown in the diagrams in Figure 1, part of the circumference of the pickleball can be over the line but technically the ball will be out because its center hit outside the line.

  Despite this rule, many players still call a ball "in" if any part of it lands on the line. In part, this is because it's difficult to tell where the center of the ball was at the time of impact. In fact, it's often hard to tell if the ball landed on the line at all, especially if you are reaching for the shot and also trying to call it. Just be aware of the actual rule, and check to see if there are any "house rules" used by the players around you.

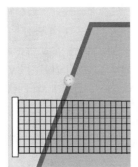 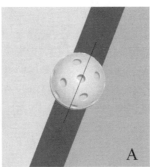 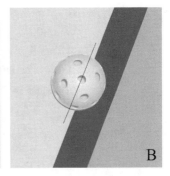

Figure 1. Calling a ball in or out depends on where the center of the ball hits the ground. Illustration A shows a ball that is ruled as IN because its center bounced on the line. Illustration B shows a ball that is OUT because its center bounced outside the line.

- During a serve, all lines on the diagonally opposite service court are good *except the line behind the non-volley zone* (otherwise known as the "kitchen"). A ball touching the non-volley zone line during a serve is a fault.[1]

- You may serve backhand as long as you serve underhand and the paddle contacts the ball below your waist.

- While serving, if you swing your paddle and miss the ball, it is a fault. However, you may drop the ball and let it hit the court surface with no fault as long as you don't swing at the ball.

- It is a fault if you step into or on the line of the non-volley zone and volley a ball. It is also a fault if you volley a ball while standing behind the non-volley zone line and *the momentum from that shot causes you to step on the line of or into the non-volley zone afterward.* This is true even if the ball is dead when your momentum causes you to enter the zone.

- It is a fault if you volley the ball and any part of your clothing, jewelry, or accessories lands in the non-volley zone (whether now attached to you or not) before the ball is dead.

- You lose the rally if you are hit by a ball in play. It doesn't matter where you are standing when the ball hits you (you can even be out of bounds). The ball might have been hit by your opponents or by your partner. And the ball doesn't have to hit your body—it can hit your clothing and this rule

---

1. This assumes that the line separating the non-volley zone from the service courts is painted so that the *back* of that line is precisely seven feet from the net. I've been told that some courts paint the *front* of this line at seven feet, and the line is then considered to be good during a serve. Evidently, some other pickleball clubs play that a ball hitting the line separating the non-volley zone from the midcourt is good, regardless of where it's painted. For tournament play, check the local rulings on the non-volley zone line before play begins.

applies. One player made it easier to understand this way: it's your fault if you are in the way of the ball.

- Tournament rules prohibit a player from catching a ball before it bounces, assuming that it would have landed out of bounds. In casual play, however, this is often done to speed up play.

- Your paddle hand is considered part of the paddle, so shots made off that hand or fingers are legal. You may not hit the ball with any other part of your arm or body.

- You may switch your paddle from one hand to the other to reach for a ball that otherwise would be a backhand shot.

- No rule prohibits doubles players from changing sides within the court after a serve and playing in each other's original territory. If your side wins the point, however, be sure you serve from the correct court.

- The partner not receiving the serve may stand anywhere on his side of the net—even out of bounds or within the receiving player's box.

- If you hit a ball that goes over the net, bounces, and then comes back over to your side *without your opponents having touched it,* it's a fault for them. This happens occasionally due to extreme backspin put on the ball.

- The net posts are out of bounds, so any ball touching a net post creates a fault. The cords running between the net and the post are considered part of the net, however, so any ball touching a cord (even outside the boundaries of the court) that then lands inside the court boundaries is good.

- While the net posts are out of bounds, you may legally hit a ball *around a net post* so that it lands within the court boundaries. There is no restriction regarding the required height of the ball in this type of shot (it does not need to be hit higher than the top of the net).

Scoring

Regulation pickleball games are played to eleven points, with the winner needing a two-point margin. When you're first learning to play pickleball, two things seem particularly hard: grasping the ball when it's tossed to you (it seems to have a life of its own and wants to be anywhere but in your hand), and, when playing doubles, keeping track of the score and calling it when serving.

It's really not that hard—calling the score, at least. (You'll get better at catching and hanging onto the ball with practice.)

With the exception of the first serve of a game,[2] each player on a doubles team will serve before the other team gets a chance. The player on the right-hand court always serves first. This player is designated as Server 1 and the other player as Server 2. Server 1 serves until the other team wins a rally. Then his partner, Server 2, serves until the other team wins a rally. At this point, the serve switches to the other team. They begin the same way: the player in the right-hand court serves first and is designated as Server 1, and so on.

Because of the need to keep track of who is serving, the server number is appended to the score that is called just before serving. Here's how it works: You call your team's score first, followed by the other team's score, and finally your server number. So if your team has 6 points, the other team has 4 points, and you're the first server on your side, you'd call the score as: "6 – 4 – 1." [Some players make this clearer by calling, "6 – 4 – server 1."]

When you are serving and your team wins a point, you switch sides on your court for the next serve. *Your server number*

---

2. The first serve of a game is played as if that server is "Server 2" for his side. Thus the first team to serve will have only one server. This arrangement helps to even the play between the teams.

doesn't change—if you were the first server, you're still the first server. When your team loses a rally, the serve will pass to your partner if you were the first server for your team or to the other team if you were your team's second server.

Here's a trick about scoring that may help if confusion arises. You can know if the score in a game should be even or odd using a method that has to do with court position. See the diagram below. When a *doubles* game begins, observe the player who serves first on each side. If play continues properly and players move as they should, a team's score will be even when the initial server is on the right (the same court he started in) and odd when that person is on the left. In *singles*, each player serves from the right-hand court when his score is even and from the left-hand court when his score is odd. Note that a score of "0" is even.

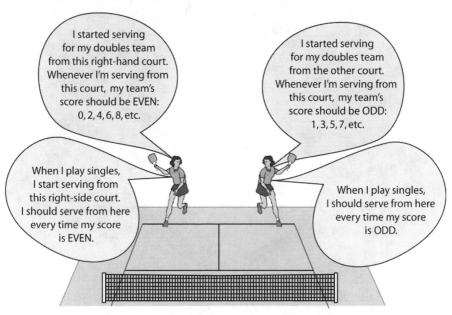

Figure 2. Knowing whether your score is even or odd helps to determine your proper serving court position. The right-hand court is known as the "even" court, and the left-hand court is known as the "odd" court.

Paddles

Paddles come in many different sizes, shapes, and materials. It's not uncommon to notice someone with a new type of paddle, be it homemade or purchased from a new vendor. The official pickleball rules do not regulate the type of material used for paddles—just their overall dimensions (the combined length and width must not exceed 23-½ inches; neither thickness nor weight are specified). Consequently, the field is still wide open for developers to try new designs, and you may want to try paddles belonging to others to find out which seems best for you.

Figure 3. Examples of different types of paddles. Note that some have larger playing surfaces and shorter handles and vice versa.

Consider these elements when choosing a paddle:

- Size of the paddle face,
- Length and circumference of the grip (it should feel comfortable when you hold it), and
- Paddle weight.

Some players feel strongly about having a light-weight paddle, claiming that such paddles allow them to hit balls faster. Some players prefer certain materials over others, stating they hit with more punch without as much effort.

The first paddles developed for pickleball were made of wood. These are still available and are the least expensive on the market. They weigh about 11 to 12 ounces.

Composite fiberglass and graphite paddles weigh less than wooden paddles, from about 6 to 9 ounces. Some models have larger paddle faces and shorter grips or the opposite.

Paddle choice seems to be a matter of personal preference. I suggest you try paddles belonging to friends, or invest in one that seems a good weight and fit and see how it does for you. The Pickleball Store (www.thepickleballstore.com) has put together a list comparing the attributes of most paddles that are currently available to help with your decision.

Balls

At the time this book was written, three brands of balls were accepted for play by the USAPA. These are manufactured by Dura, Cosom® and Jugs, and are available in either white or yellow. Dura balls are used for outdoor tournament play because they are thicker and harder, making them last longer. Two other balls are available from Pickle-Ball®, Inc. One bears their name and the other is from Singapore. Both of these balls are rotationally molded, which means they are seamless, and the holes are drilled afterward.

The differences in balls can be significant. Balls like the Dura have a greater number of smaller holes; others, such as the Cosom Fun Ball or Jugs ball, have larger holes, which can cause more windage, making the play a little slower and causing the balls to fly less high or far. The smaller holes of the Dura ball allow it to fly faster and farther and also make it capable of attaining greater spin. The balls from Pickle-Ball, Inc., and those from Singapore are very similar, although the Singapore ball tends to be a little softer and slower.

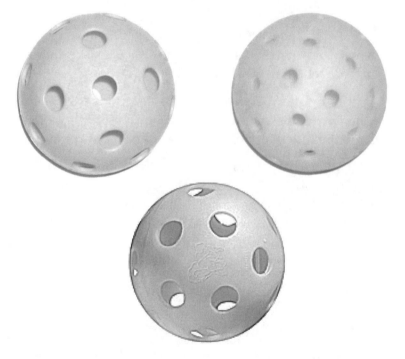

Figure 4. Cosom ball (left); Dura ball (right); Jugs ball (bottom).

The Court

A pickleball court is 20 feet wide by 44 feet long, whether playing singles or doubles (the same dimensions as a badminton court). The top of the net should be 36 inches from the ground at the posts and 34 inches at the center. The non-volley zone ("kitchen") is marked by a line 7 feet from the net on each side of the court. The 15-foot area between the non-volley zone and the baseline is divided by a line into two equal rectangles that are 10 feet wide. At least three feet on each end and two feet on each side should be included for player movement outside the court boundaries.

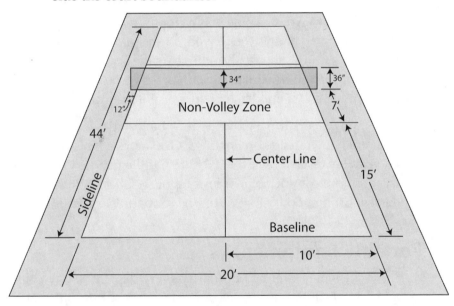

Figure 5. The dimensions and areas of a regulation pickleball court.

The type of playing surface is not specified in the rules. It must be hard enough to allow the plastic ball to bounce. I've seen games played on hard outdoor courts and wooden floors, and I understand that some facilities have carpeted courts.

Clothing and Other Equipment

Many pickleball players use no other equipment besides good court or cross-training shoes (these are important), socks with cushioned soles and heels, loose-fitting clothing, sunblock and a visor or sunglasses (if you're playing outside), and a paddle.

If you can't find a pair of shoes that is suited to your particular court conditions, or if those change, I recommend a pair of cross-training shoes that can be used for many different sports. When I interviewed Doisey Landry for this book, she mentioned that she and her husband discovered pickleball when they moved to Arizona. She was eager to try this new sport, but the moving van hadn't yet arrived, so she played her first game with the "wrong" shoes. She still bears the scar she earned while sliding on the court. Needless to say, she now uses the appropriate shoes and hasn't had a problem since.

Some players use a glove to get a better grip, especially when playing outside on hot days. Grip tapes are also available and can be applied over the existing paddle handle to make it larger, more comfortable, or less slippery. Check with your local sporting goods store or online for paddle accessories.

Portable Equipment

Pickleball is gaining popularity every day, but many cities and schools do not yet have courts designed for its play. Yet you can play this game almost anywhere there is a flat surface with enough room.

Pickleball can be played both indoors and out. Portable nets and water-filled standards are available that make playing anywhere easier. A gymnasium floor can be taped off for pickleball courts. Because a badminton court is the same size as a pickleball court, you can simply lower the net to the proper pickleball height. (Note that the "short service line" in badminton is 6'6" away from the net instead of 7'0", but it works in a pinch.) A tennis court will also do, but the center of a tennis net is two inches higher than a regulation pickleball net. Simply tape or chalk lines on the tennis court and you're ready to go.

If you're building new court space, orient the long side in the north-south direction. This avoids having players stare directly into the sun in the early morning or late afternoon.

A note about converting tennis courts for pickleball use: the pad for a regulation tennis court is 60 x 120 feet, which is precisely four times the size of a regulation pickleball court (30 x 60 feet). This means you can create four pickleball courts within the space of one tennis court.

Chapter 2

Grips, Body Positions, and Strokes

Pickleball is similar to several other paddle and racquet sports. Those of you who have played tennis, racquetball, table tennis, paddleball, or other similar sports will be able to bring many of those skills to the pickleball court.

As with those other sports, you must combine a series of individual elements to make a shot. The way you hold the paddle and how you stand and move on the court influence where your shot will go. Much of this seems to come naturally to a novice pickleball player, but it's wise to learn the correct way to play before learning anything incorrectly and having to "unlearn" it later.

It's worth noting that improper techniques will make it harder for you to improve your game, and that incorrect play may also lead to injury. The correct way to do things may feel awkward or strange at first, but it's worth taking the time to learn the right way to hit the ball and move on the court. Your body will be happier, and your game will be better.

The four basic elements of the physical game are:

- How you hold the paddle,
- The paddle angle at the time of impact,
- Your body position before, during, and after the impact, and
- The motion and direction of your swing, including the follow through.

Holding the Paddle

Having a grip on the paddle that works for you and for the type of shot you are making is essential to playing well. Your grip is an extension of your arm and hand.

The word "grip" might lead you to believe that you should hold the handle tightly. Don't do that. Hold the handle just firmly enough that you don't lose it during play. You can grip more tightly at the moment of impact with the ball, if you wish, and then return to your regular grip.

Ask five pickleball players what they do and you will typically get five different answers. Which is right? In general, whatever works best for you. However, this chapter presents guidelines for those of you who haven't played paddle or racquet sports before and for those who are experiencing pain or finding it difficult to get the ball to go where you want it to.

Some of the pickleball players I interviewed use one grip for all strokes and simply vary the paddle angle to change the direction of the shot. Other players said they feel more comfortable switching their grip to a different paddle position for backhand shots.

Sue Gardiner, a medal-winning player and pickleball teacher, says it is important to change your grip from forehand to backhand in order to reduce the possibility of repetitive motion injury. Besides this, one reason to use both forehand and backhand grips is that your strokes will likely be more effective. Other grips, borrowed from tennis play, might be useful in pickleball, although most players don't seem to need more than the two presented here. However, if you want to try other grips as you become a better player, remember that any new grip should either improve your control and/or comfort.

The difference between the forehand and backhand grips is the angle at which the paddle rests in the hand. Changing this angle allows you to present a flat paddle face to the ball no matter where the ball is in relation to your body. If you always use a forehand grip on the backhand side, for instance, you might slice under the ball unintentionally, reducing your control on the shot.

The Forehand Grip

The basic grip described here is comfortable for most players. (For those of you with tennis backgrounds, it is similar to the eastern forehand.) This grip may be used for overheads and volley shots as well as forehands.

The easiest way to find this grip is to hold the paddle in front of you in your non-paddle hand so that the handle is toward you and the faces of the paddle are perpendicular to the ground. Adjust the paddle, if necessary, so that you can see only the outer edge of the frame. Now shake hands with the handle. Center the "V" formed between your forefinger and thumb over an imaginary line running from the edge of the frame along the top of the handle.

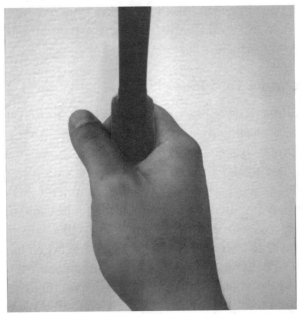

Figure 6. Top view of the forehand grip (right-handed).

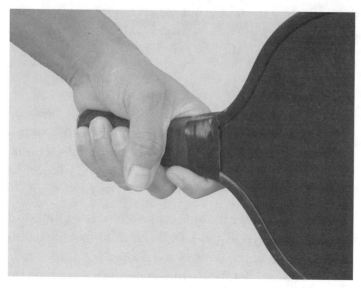

Figure 7. Side view of the forehand grip (left-handed).

The butt of the handle should be about even with the edge of your hand and should project approximately half an inch from your fingers. Grip the handle firmly, but not tightly. Most people wrap their thumbs around the handle so that it touches or overlaps their other fingers.

Extending Your Index Finger

Some players like to keep their index or first two fingers straight, placing these on the back face of the paddle. This practice probably stems from table tennis techniques that are designed to give more control when executing spin shots. Most of the players I spoke with don't recommend this practice. They say it stiffens your hold on the paddle and seems to take power away from the shot. Those who like to extend a finger on the back of the paddle face, however, argue that they achieve better control, greater spin, and comfort. I say that you should do what seems right for you. If you use finger extension and find that you aren't able to get enough power in your shots, try removing the finger and see what happens. If you don't extend a finger and are having trouble with spins, see if placing a finger on the back of the paddle helps.

The Backhand Grip

This grip is nearly the same as the forehand, but the paddle is rotated clockwise just a bit so that the "V" between your thumb and fingers rests over the corner of the handle between the right side and top. (This is similar to the eastern backhand grip in tennis.)

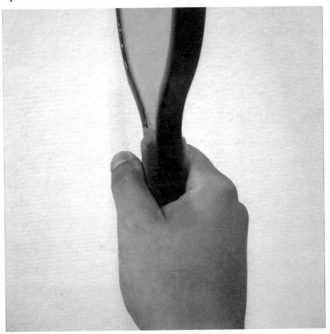

Figure 8. The backhand grip (right-handed).

To achieve this grip, start with the forehand grip described earlier. Hold the paddle so that the top edge points to the 12 o'clock position. Leaving your hand in the same position, loosen your grip, and use your other hand to turn the paddle clockwise so that its top edge points to the 1 o'clock position for a right-hander or 11 o'clock for a left-handed player.

The reason for the slight turn is to close the paddle face just a little on your backhand shots, prohibiting them from traveling too high over the net. Using this grip means that you don't have to turn your arm to achieve the same result, reducing stress on the muscles and ligaments in your forearm and elbow.

Very few players use a two-handed style: the grip of the main hand remains the same, but the second hand grips above the main hand, adding power to the stroke when it's needed. While effective in tennis, most players find this is not necessary in pickleball since power isn't really required for most shots. It's also far more difficult to execute since the handle of a pickleball paddle is so much shorter than the handle of a tennis racquet.

Paddle Angles

The face of the paddle can be angled in three ways, depending on the type of shot you wish to make. Understanding the differences between these paddle angles and their effects upon the shots will help you determine when to use them and why.

Certain types of shots demand a particular paddle angle to work well. Additionally, it's important to think about where the ball is in relation to the height of the net, as this, too, will determine the angle needed to direct the ball properly.

Flat Face

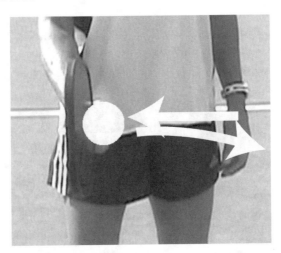

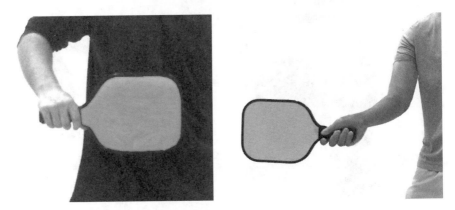

Figure 9. Paddle face in the flat position.

The paddle is not angled either up or down. The face is kept parallel to the net. A ball hit with a flat face will travel in a relatively straight direction, eventually dropping due to gravity.

When you want to hit a ball that will travel just over the net, keep the paddle face flat. Use it to keep the ball low during forehand and backhand drives and serves as well as some volley shots.

Open Face

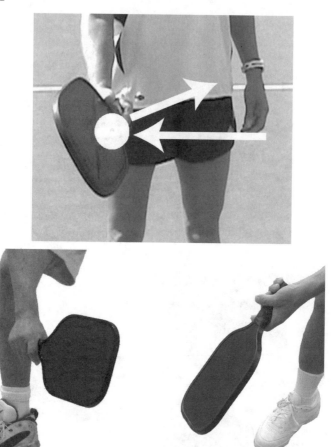

Figure 10. Paddle face in the open position.

The paddle is angled so the face points up to about 30 degrees from vertical. The amount of openness varies depending on the height of the ball when you hit it. If the ball is below the top of the net when you hit it (either before or after a bounce), open the paddle face slightly to direct the ball upward to clear the net.

Use an open paddle face for serves, lobs, half volleys, some spin shots, and other strokes made when the ball is low.

Closed Face

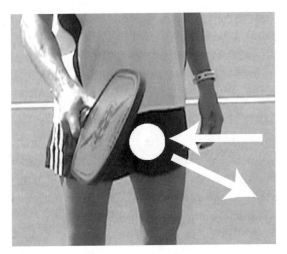

Figure 11. Paddle face in the closed position.

The paddle is angled so the face points down to about 30 degrees from vertical. If the ball is higher than the net when you hit it, close the face slightly to keep the ball down so your opponents don't smash it back at you. Also close this paddle angle when hitting a ball that comes above your shoulders to ensure that it doesn't go out of bounds.

This angle is used for smashes, high volleys, and some spin shots.

Body Positions and Strokes

In general, all swings should begin from the ready position (see Figure 12) whenever possible. Good swings require a proper backswing, contact, and then follow through to be effective. The arm that is not swinging the paddle is used to maintain balance.

Watch a better player sometime and you'll notice that his head stays quite still during most swings. When he's finished the follow through, his paddle returns to a spot about waist high in front of him, and he pivots to face the opponent who is returning the ball. He also usually centers himself in the width of the court (or his half of it in doubles), giving himself the most opportunity to reach a ball, no matter where it goes. Emulate this style and your game should improve.

Several of the people I talked to stressed the importance of bending your knees to hit a ball rather than bending over from the waist. Bending your knees allows you to respond more quickly to the ball coming toward you and adds power to your swing. It also keeps your eyes more level with the ball as it heads toward you and is easier on your back.

Several physics principles are at work when you hit a ball returned from an opponent. First, that ball is traveling at a certain speed, with a certain amount of spin (or not), at a certain direction. Gravity is in this equation, too, along with any wind. If you simply stand by and let a ball hit your paddle, it will bounce off with about half of its original force. The speed of your return shot is derived from adding that half of your opponent's force to the amount of energy you put into your stroke at the point of impact.[3] What does all this mean? The harder your opponent's shot, the greater the force of your shot will be with the same amount of effort on your part.

---

3. Derived from Vic Braden's studies on the physics of tennis, *Vic's Tips,* http://www.vicbraden.com/vics1.html#how.

The Ready Position

Face your opponents with your knees slightly bent, approximately shoulder-width apart, leaning forward just a little. Remain alert but relaxed, and keep your weight evenly distributed on both feet. Hold the paddle in front of you between your waist and chest, straight forward or angled toward the backhand, keeping you ready for fast volleys that head straight toward you where a forehand stroke isn't possible.

Figure 12. The ready position.

Return to the ready position between shots whenever possible. If you don't, you may not be able to react as quickly and may not have time to return your best shot. Always try to anticipate where your opponent's shot is headed when you move out of the ready position to return a shot. Don't let your paddle drop down toward your knees. Keep it raised and ready to go, and your reaction times will be better.

When to Hit the Ball

A bouncing ball rises from the ground in a curved motion and then drops back down to bounce again. At what point in that arc should your paddle contact a bouncing ball?

Issues surrounding the answer have to do with the physics of the ball's motion, how that motion interacts with your paddle and the motion of your swing, as well as the trajectory of typical swings, whether or not they will send the ball over the net and, if so, how the ball will move.

Hitting after a Bounce: Typically, the best place to hit a groundstroke is on the rise from the ground when the ball is between your knees and your waist.

Figure 13. The best place to hit a ball after a bounce is on the rise, between your knees and waist.

If you hit it sooner (when the ball is lower than your knees), you'll have to open the paddle face in order to ensure that the ball clears the net. This can cause the ball to rise higher than desired, and could result in your opponent smashing it back to you.

Waiting until the ball has passed the apex and is headed down again is easier when you're new to the game since it gives you a longer time react and hit the ball. The longer you wait, however, the more time your opponents have to prepare for your next shot.

If you hit a bouncing ball when it's *above* your waist, close the paddle face a little to keep the ball low so it won't be smashed back at you.

In terms of where to hit a groundstroke in relation to your body, the ball should be opposite your forward hip for a forehand and ahead of your forward hip for a backhand.

Hitting a Volley: Hit volleys between waist and shoulder height, and keep your paddle closer to your body than when you hit groundstroke forehands or backhands. Generally, volleys require little backswing and don't have a significant follow through after you hit the ball. Hit the volley as a "punch" off your paddle from in front of your body.

Figure 14. Hit the volley between waist and shoulder height when the ball is in front of your body. Be sure you are out of the non-volley zone when you hit the volley.

Hitting a Smash: Strive to hit the overhead smash at the full extension of the paddle, if possible, by extending your arm and shoulder into the stroke. Hit the ball when it is roughly in line with your front foot. Don't wait much longer than that because the ball will be more likely to go into the net.

Figure 15. Hit the overhead with your arm fully extended when the ball is in line with your front foot. Be sure you are out of the non-volley zone when you hit an overhead smash.

The Forehand Groundstroke

When you hit a bouncing ball using a forehand stroke, use a forehand grip and keep the paddle face fairly flat (parallel to the net). This helps to keep the ball low as it crosses the net. You can put quite a bit of power into a forehand stroke since the low trajectory of the ball helps to keep it in bounds.

Start your backswing as you move into position and shift your weight to your back foot.

After you hit the ball, let the paddle follow its flight.

From the ready position, turn toward the side where the ball will come.

Align your body parallel to the ball's flight. Swing "through the ball" as you step into the shot. Contact the ball in line with your front foot.

As your weight shifts to your forward foot, bring your back foot forward and move toward your next position.

Figure 16. The forehand stroke.

From the ready position, turn to the side where the ball will land so that you are facing the sideline. Some players pivot on the balls of their feet or step onto their back foot to accomplish this. More of your weight should be on your back foot at this point. Draw your paddle back and upward, keeping your elbow bent slightly, and extend your other arm toward the net for balance.

Keep your eyes on the ball and your head steady. As the ball comes toward you, step forward, shifting your weight to your front foot, and swing the paddle through to contact the ball. Hit the ball when it is in line with your front foot. Keep your elbow bent slightly throughout the swing. The paddle face should be flat or angled open just a little at the moment of contact.

During the swing, lean into the ball and follow through. Leaning into the ball will keep the paddle head vertical at the point of impact—otherwise the face may open up.

Finish with the follow through: continue swinging the paddle in the intended direction of the ball, reaching out as far as possible in that direction. Your shoulders should automatically

Keep your eyes on the ball as it comes to you.

Use the proper grip (forehand or backhand).

Use your non-paddle arm to help keep your balance.

Keep your knees slightly bent after you pivot.

After you start your forward swing, step in with your forward foot.

Figure 17. The backswing.

Your head should be steady and eyes on the ball.

Don't let the paddle head dip or rise too much, and keep the face flat or angled open just a little.

Shift weight to your forward foot as you hit the ball.

Keep feet at least shoulder width apart for balance as you swing.

Figure 18. Contacting the ball.

pivot so that they are facing the net at the end of
the swing. Your forward
knee should still be bent
to keep your balance and
help you return quickly to
the ready position.

Use a hard forehand
drive to your opponent's
forehand or backhand
side to keep him deep in
his court. Aiming your
shots cross-court will give
you more room to stay in
bounds and will keep
your opponent running
and on the defensive.

*Follow the path
of the ball with
your paddle.*

*Swing rear foot
through and prepare
for next shot.*

Figure 19. The follow through.

Possible Problems with the Forehand Groundstroke

- **Walking or running into the shot.** If you are moving forward when you start a forehand swing, your body may not
  be in the proper position to achieve the backswing needed
  to execute the shot properly. Additionally, the momentum
  of your forward movement will be added to the power of
  the shot, so you should hit the ball a little softer to keep it in
  bounds. Lastly, you may not be able to follow through as
  well as with a shot taken from a steady position.

- **Not taking enough preparation swing or follow through.**
  Be sure to start your swing early enough to allow you a
  proper backswing. As you start your foreswing, don't think
  of the moment of contact with the ball as the end of the
  swing. Instead, think about sweeping your paddle right
  through the ball and into your follow through.

- **The ball travels too far (out of bounds).** The face of your paddle is probably open (not parallel to the net) or you may be waiting too long to hit the ball. Keep the face of the paddle flat, and try to contact the ball when it is even with your forward foot, before it reaches the apex of its upward motion.

- **The ball doesn't go far enough.** Step into your swing and be sure to follow through after contacting the ball.

- **The ball always goes to the right or the left.** Make sure your body is turned all the way to the sideline on your backswing and when you hit the ball. Follow through in the target direction.

- **Very little power in your hit.** If you contact the ball too late, you'll lose power. Make sure your body is positioned so you're facing the sideline and step into the swing. Your weight should be on your front foot when the paddle hits the ball. You might be bending your wrist as you contact the ball. Keep your wrist firm without bending through the entire stroke. Check that your grip is firm and that you don't lose power because the paddle wobbles in your hand.

- **The ball always goes into the net.** Try opening the paddle face slightly to pick the ball up a bit more on the return stroke, or change your grip so that the paddle face is automatically a little more open.

The Backhand Groundstroke

When you hit a bouncing ball using a backhand stroke, use a backhand grip and keep the paddle face fairly flat (parallel to the net). This helps to keep the ball low as it crosses the net. You can put quite a bit of power into a backhand stroke since the low trajectory of the ball helps to keep it in bounds.

Start your backswing as you move into position and shift your weight to your back foot.

After you hit the ball, let the paddle follow its flight.

From the ready position, turn toward the side where the ball will come.

Align your body parallel to the ball's flight. Swing "through the ball" as you step into the shot. Contact the ball in line with your front foot.

As your weight shifts to your forward foot, bring your back foot up as you move to the ready position.

Figure 20. The backhand stroke.

From the ready position, turn to the side where the ball will land so that you are facing the sideline. Some players pivot on the balls of their feet or step onto their back foot to accomplish this. More of your weight should be on your back foot at this point. Draw your paddle back and upward, keeping your elbow bent slightly. Keep your other arm out to the side for balance.

Keep your eyes on the ball as it comes to you.

Use the proper backhand grip.

Keep your knees slightly bent after you pivot.

Your non-paddle arm helps you keep your balance.

As you start the forward swing, step in with your forward foot.

Figure 21. The backswing.

Keep your head steady and eyes on the ball.

Keep the paddle face flat and keep the head even with or higher than the handle.

Shift weight to your forward foot as you hit the ball.

Keep feet at least shoulder width apart for balance as you swing.

Figure 22. Contacting the ball.

Keep your eyes on the ball and your head steady. As the ball comes toward you, step forward, shifting your weight to your front foot, and swing the paddle through to contact the ball. Hit the ball when it is in line with your front foot. Keep your elbow bent slightly throughout the swing. The paddle face should be flat or angled open just a little at the moment of contact.

During the swing, lean into the ball since this will keep the paddle head vertical at the point of impact—otherwise the face may open up. Keep your wrist locked and your arm straight at the point of impact. Keep your head down and steady all the way through the stroke.

Finish with the follow through: continue swinging the paddle in the intended direction of the ball, reaching out as far as possible in that direction. Your shoulders should automatically pivot so that they are facing the net at the end of the swing. Your forward knee should still be

Follow the path of the ball with your paddle.

Swing rear foot through and prepare for next shot.

Figure 23. The follow through.

bent to keep your balance and help you return quickly to the ready position.

Use a hard forehand drive to your opponent's forehand or backhand side to keep him deep in his court. Aiming your shots cross-court will give you more room to stay in bounds and will keep your opponent running and on the defensive.

Possible Problems with the Backhand Groundstroke

- **Not taking enough preparation swing or follow through.** Be sure to start your swing early enough to allow you a proper backswing. As you start your foreswing, don't think of the moment of contact with the ball as the end of the swing. Instead, think about sweeping your paddle right through the ball and into your follow through.

- **The ball travels too far (out of bounds).** The face of your paddle is probably open (not parallel to the net) or you may be waiting too long to hit the ball. Keep the face of the paddle flat, and try to contact the ball when it is even with your forward foot, before it reaches the apex of its upward motion.

- **The ball doesn't go far enough.** Step into your swing and be sure to follow through after contacting the ball.

- **The ball always goes to the right or the left.** Make sure your body is turned all the way to the sideline on your backswing and when you hit the ball. Follow through in the target direction. Keep your wrist straight (don't let it flex) when the paddle hits the ball.

- **Very little power in your hit.** If you contact the ball too late, you'll lose power. Make sure your body is positioned so you're facing the sideline and step into the swing. Your weight should be on your front foot when the paddle hits the ball. You might be bending your wrist as you contact the ball. Keep your wrist firm without bending through the entire stroke. Check that your grip is firm and that you don't lose power because your paddle wobbles in your hand. Loss of power is most noticeable with backhand drives. Using a two-handed backhand stroke is not recommended for pickleball, however. Unlike tennis, the pickleball paddle is extremely light in weight, so the two-handed grip really isn't necessary.

- **The ball always goes into the net.** Try opening the paddle face slightly to pick the ball up a bit more on the return stroke, or change your grip so that the paddle face is automatically a little more open.

- **Your arm or elbow hurts when swinging backhand.** If you don't already use it, try changing to the backhand grip. If you do use that grip, check with a medical professional as it may be tennis elbow. See more about tennis elbow on page 72.

The Serve

The underhand serve in pickleball doesn't allow for many aces, but I still consider it to be the most important shot because every rally begins with a serve. Concentrate on making sure that your serve clears the net and lands in the correct diagonal service court. The best serves are made deep to the center or backhand side of the service court, keeping your opponent back (because the double-bounce rule says he must let the ball bounce before they hit it).

Don't neglect your backswing or follow through. The backswing adds power to your serve, allowing you to hit it further and harder into your opponent's back court, and the follow through will ensure that the ball travels where you want it to go.

In general, most players' serves are very much like their forehand drives. The paddle angle is flat (parallel to the net), which keeps the ball low as it crosses the net. You can put quite a lot of power into the serve since the low trajectory of the ball helps to keep it in bounds. It's fine, however, if you're not comfortable with a low, hard shot and want to hit a softer, higher serve since your opponents must let the ball bounce before they can return it. In fact, a good change of pace is to serve a high, deep ball every now and then.

During the serve, your paddle must contact the ball *at or below* your waist, your back foot *must remain behind the baseline*, and your back foot *must be in contact with the ground* at the time the paddle hits the ball. Although the rules allow you to have one foot inside the baseline during a serve, it's best to keep both feet outside the baseline when serving. The extra foot or so that you gain by having one foot inside doesn't help your serve that much, and anything you can do to avoid foot faults is good. Besides, you'll want to wait behind the baseline until your opponents have returned the ball to accommodate the double-bounce rule, so it just makes sense to start there.

Forehand Serve

With both feet behind the baseline, turn toward your paddle arm so that you are facing the sideline. Transfer your weight to your back foot as you draw your paddle back and upward, keeping your elbow bent slightly.

Extend your other hand holding the ball toward the net and *position the ball in line with your target—in the direction you wish the ball to travel.* This is important, since the placement of the ball when you hit it helps to determine the direction of its flight.

Turn your body so your shoulders point to the diagonal service court.

When you start your foreswing, drop the ball and swing "through it" as you step into the shot. Contact the ball in line with your front foot.

After you hit the ball, let the paddle follow its flight.

Hold the ball about even with your forward foot and point it toward your target.

As your weight shifts to your forward foot, bring your back foot forward and move toward your next position.

Figure 24. The forehand serve.

When the paddle reaches the apex of your backswing, drop the ball.[4] Keep your eyes on the ball and your head steady. Step

4. Some players toss the ball into the air and hit it on its way back down. Most of the players I spoke with don't recommend this, however. In a couple of instances, in fact, players have suddenly developed difficulty controlling their serves after they'd been playing for a while. When they stopped tossing the ball, their control problems disappeared.

forward (being careful not to step onto or over the baseline), shifting your weight to your front foot, and swing the paddle through to contact the ball. Keep your elbow bent slightly throughout the swing. Depending on the angle of your stroke, the paddle face should be flat or angled slightly open at the moment it contacts the ball.

Finish the swing with the follow through: continue swinging the paddle in the intended direction of the ball, reaching out and upward as far as possible. Keep your forward knee bent to keep your balance and help you return quickly to the ready position.

Backhand Serve

A few players like to hit backhand serves. These are harder to perfect, partly because the backhand has less power than the forehand and because getting the ball to land in the correct service court can be more difficult. However, some players find that it's easier to impart spin with a backhand stroke—in fact, it's hard to serve backhand and *not* spin the ball—and they find the spin makes their serves harder to return well.

In general, the process of serving backhand is the same as forehand, except that your arms are crossed while you take your backswing and hold the ball out in front of you. The rest of the stroke is virtually the same as the backhand groundstroke.

Make sure the paddle contacts the ball at or below your waist—any higher and it will be a fault. When serving backhand, it may be necessary to bend over a little more than usual to ensure the point of contact is low enough.

Possible Problems with the Serve (Forehand and Backhand)

- **The ball goes into the net.** Try hitting the ball a little sooner—don't wait until the ball is too low. If you do hit the ball lower, open up the paddle face a little more to angle the ball slightly higher.

- **The ball doesn't always land in the service court.** Make sure you're holding the ball in line with your target. Execute a good follow through, so that your paddle points to the direction of your shot. Keep your eye on the ball.

- **Hitting the ball too early or too late.** You may be releasing the ball poorly. Concentrate first on preparing for your stroke with a good backswing. Then release the ball. Finally think about hitting the ball, concentrating not on the actual contact but rather on stroking *through* the ball, finishing with a good follow through in the direction you want the ball to travel.

- **The ball goes too far.** The face of your paddle is probably open (not parallel to the net) or you may be waiting too long to hit the ball. Keep the face of the paddle flat, and try to contact the ball just below the level of your waist.

- **The ball doesn't go far enough.** Step into your swing and be sure to follow through after contacting the ball. Check the angle of your paddle to make sure it is flat or only slightly open.

- **The ball goes to the right or the left.** Make sure your body is turned all the way to the sideline on your swing and when you hit the ball. You should hit the ball when it is even with your front foot.

- **(Using a backhand serve) Very little power in your hit.** The backhand swing is generally not as powerful as the forehand. Because of this, you may need to add a little more power in order to ensure that the ball travels over the net and as far as desired (and you can't use two hands even if you wanted to because one of them is holding the ball). If you contact the ball too late, you'll lose power because you'll have to open up the face to get the ball over the net. Make sure your body is positioned so you're facing the sideline, and step into the swing. Your weight should be on your front foot when the paddle hits the ball.

The Volley

A good offense begins with good net position—with you (and your partner) just behind the non-volley zone—and the ability to hit volleys well. Volleying is hitting the ball before it has a chance to bounce. Having a good volley is crucial to being good at the game of pickleball, and it's the volley that makes pickleball such a fun, fast-paced game. While you can hit a volley any time the ball has not yet bounced, *the best volleys are made when the ball is above the net and you can hit it in a downward direction.*

When you volley, you are not trying to smash the ball back. Rather, you just need to stop the motion of the ball and send it back over the net, trying more to direct the hit than to put a lot of power behind it. When you volley, keep facing the net or the opponent who is sending the ball your way—don't turn sideways as with a groundstroke. You also don't really have time to execute a complete backswing, and it's best *not* to follow through with most volleys since your forward momentum might carry you into the non-volley zone.

Punch the paddle forward to meet the ball in front of your body. Try to meet the volley above net height, between your waist and shoulders.

If possible, the volley stroke should proceed from high to low (just the opposite of the equivalent groundstroke).

Figure 25. Forehand and backhand volley examples.

Keep your wrist firm (don't let it flex or wobble) during the volley. The volley doesn't have a standard follow through. Instead, straighten your paddle arm at the moment of impact and continue punching down and through the ball. Keep your head level and your eyes on the ball, even after you hit it, as this will clue you where to move and where your paddle should go, depending on how your opponent appears to be returning the ball.

You should still try to return to the ready position between volleys, but keep your paddle slightly higher—about chest height. Sometimes the volleys go so fast that you don't have time to get back to the ready position. When you know this will occur, you can try using a forehand or backhand sweep (see "Backhand and Forehand Sweeps" on page 55) to volley a very fast shot.

If you must volley a ball that is below net height, open the paddle face slightly to help the ball to clear the net. Don't angle it too much because that will send the ball too high, giving your opponents the opportunity to smash the ball back. Bend your knees to get down under the ball rather than bending over, and try to keep the face of the paddle and the handle parallel to the ground. This will help to keep your return shots in bounds and headed in the direction you intend them to go.

Possible Problems with the Volley

- **The ball travels too far (out of bounds).** Shorten your backswing and/or your follow through. Instead of using either of those, punch the ball back, keeping the ball centered on the paddle face, if possible.

- **The ball travels too high.** If you're hitting a volley that is below the level of the net, keep the paddle face flatter and bend your knees to get your paddle to the level of the ball.

The Overhead Smash

When your opponent returns a high ball (at or above your shoulders), you have the opportunity to execute a "smash" shot. When hit properly, you will generally hit from front- to midcourt, and the ball will head downward. Sometimes the best target will be your opponent's feet or body, an open area, or just inside a sideline (the most dangerous placement since it requires greater skill to keep the ball in bounds).

It's important to keep the paddle angle closed (with the top of the paddle angled downward) when executing this shot. If you don't close the face, this shot will most likely travel too high and head out of bounds. Don't close the face too much, however, as this will put the ball into the net.

Turn sideways and point at the ball above your head as it descends. Keep your eyes on the ball.

Keep the paddle face closed when contacting the ball.

Continue to follow through, with your paddle following the trajectory of the ball.

Bring the paddle up behind your head, keeping your elbow bent and weight on your back foot.

Extend your arm fully, keeping your eyes on the ball. Your weight shifts to your front foot.

As your weight shifts to your forward foot, bring your back foot forward and move toward your next position.

Figure 26. The overhead smash or slam.

You'll need time to get under the ball and prepare a good backswing for the overhead smash. When your paddle contacts the ball is important for the shot to travel properly.

Move into position under the ball, angling your body slightly sideways to the net, and swing the paddle up and behind your head, with your elbow bent and slightly higher than the paddle. Reach your other arm up and point to the ball, helping to keep your eyes focused on it as you continue your swing.[5] At this point, your back should be slightly arched, and your weight should be on your back foot.

Lead the movement of your arm with your elbow as you begin your forward swing. The paddle will follow and rise to meet the ball in the air as your weight shifts toward your forward foot. Try to hit the ball when it is about a foot in front of your paddle-side shoulder at the peak of your swing. The smash is one of the few pickleball shots where your wrist should *not* remain stiff through the contact of the ball. Instead, *snap your wrist* so the paddle angles down at the moment of contact, helping to keep the ball down.

Figure 27. Turn your paddle and stroke the right side of the ball to add spin to your overhead smash.

Continue with the follow through, bringing your paddle down and across your body as you step forward so that your weight is now fully on your forward foot. Keep your balance by stepping up with your other foot and bringing your paddle back to the ready position.

Pointing to the ball with your non-paddle hand as the ball descends helps to ensure a hit by keeping your eye on the ball (and thinking about the ball, not the shot). However, you should not point immediately: *keep your chin up* and your eye on the ball. Rotate your shoulders. Coil your swing and *then* rotate your other *elbow* toward the ball. Then point your finger at the ball, and take an *easy swing*.

5. One player mentioned that pointing his finger helps him discern how close the ball is as a reference point of size, helping him judge when it is time to swing. Against the sky, he says, with no reference point, it's almost impossible for your brain to understand how close or far something really is.

The last part of that statement is important: even though the name of this stroke is "smash," this doesn't mean you should put every ounce of strength you have behind it. In fact, if you do, the ball will most likely land in the net. It's better to execute a *well-placed* smash, aimed at your opponent's feet, that will be hard for him to return.

You can add sidespin to your overhead stroke to make the ball swerve both before and after the bounce. Change your grip slightly so that the paddle is angled a little at the moment of impact. Send the overhead smash wide, across the court if you can, directly at your opponent's feet or body, or deep down the center of the court.

The smash can only be used with high balls, either from a bounce or volley, or with lobs, especially those that aren't executed well and fall short. If you can devise a game plan that causes your opponent to use defensive lobs, you'll have more opportunity to smash the ball back.

Possible Problems with the Overhead Smash

- **The smash doesn't have much power.** Make sure your back is arched a little and that you are turned slightly to the side (about halfway between forward and sideways). During the swing, turn your upper body and shift your weight toward your front foot. Swing the paddle "through" the ball, using a snap of the wrist at the point of contact to add power and keep the ball moving downward as you continue to step forward.

- **The ball travels out of bounds.** Most likely, you hit the ball when it is over your head. Hit the ball when it is about a foot in front of you. Also, don't forget to snap your wrist when hitting the ball. This closes the face slightly, ensuring a downward direction, keeping the ball in bounds.

- **The ball goes into the net.** Don't put quite so much power into the shot. Concentrate on directing the shot where you want it to go—not on powering it there. *Be sure to follow through,* continuing your motion in the direction you want the ball to travel.

The Lob

This shot is used when you need to drive your opponent away from the net and back to his baseline (the offensive lob) or when you need time to recover from a shot that has forced you out of position (off to a sideline, for example—the defensive lob). The lob should travel over your opponent's head just inside the baseline.

Forehand and backhand lobs are executed almost exactly like forehand and backhand drives, but with an open paddle face, less power, and a higher follow through.

Keep your head steady and your eyes on the ball. Your paddle face should be open to lift the ball, but not so much that the shot falls short.[6]

---

6. That's the danger with the lob. Bill Booth is adamant that the lob should be used *very sparingly.* He says that most lobs don't go as planned and good opponents simply smash them back at you, even from the backcourt. He suggests using the lob only when your opponents are at the non-volley zone line and only when you don't have a better shot.

Start your backswing as you move into position and shift your weight to your back foot.

Continue to follow through quite high, with your paddle following the trajectory of the ball.

From the ready position, turn toward the side where the ball will come.

Align your body parallel to the ball's flight. Swing "through the ball" as you step into the shot. Contact the ball in line with your front foot.

As your weight shifts to your forward foot, bring your back foot forward and move toward your next position.

Figure 28. The lob.

The lob is most often used as a defensive shot, used to buy yourself time, especially if you have been forced to a back corner of the court or any place where you are out of position and need a bit more time to get back. However, it can also be used offensively to send your opponents away from the non-volley zone to their back court.

The offensive lob is best sent over your opponent's backhand side since he will find it difficult to smash a lob back while moving diagonally backward to reach the ball.

For a defensive lob, make the shot slow since this gives you more time to move up to the non-volley zone. Sending the ball cross-court will make it travel a longer distance (which takes even longer) and is safer because there is less probability that the shot will land out of bounds.

Possible Problems with the Lob

- **The ball doesn't travel far enough.** Start your swing sooner. Put a little more power into your swing, hitting up and through the ball. Make sure the paddle face is open. Carry the ball on your follow through, which should extend further than with a drive shot.

- **The ball doesn't travel high enough.** Open the paddle face.

- **The wind carries/stops my shot.** Take note of the direction and strength of the wind and alter the power and angle of your shot accordingly.

Drop Shot and Drop Volley

The drop shot and drop volley are difficult to master but are worth practicing since they can win points when executed well.

Both are soft strokes, made with a flat or slightly open paddle angle, either forehand or backhand. The drop shot is hit off the bounce, generally from the back- or center-court area; the drop volley is hit before the bounce and is usually done from midcourt or at the non-volley zone.

These shots should just clear the net and then drop into the non-volley zone. They are used most often when your opponents are in their back court and may not be able to reach a ball landing so close to the net. Angle the ball away from them, if possible.

Figure 29. The drop shot and drop volley travel just over the net into the non-volley zone.

Practice these shots. You don't want to angle the ball too high or your opponents will smash it back at you; don't send the shot too low or the ball won't make it over the net.

Possible Problems with the Drop Shot and Drop Volley

- **The ball travels too far (doesn't land in the non-volley zone).** The face of your paddle is probably open (not parallel to the net) or you may be waiting too long to hit the ball. For a drop shot, keep the face of the paddle flat and try to contact the ball before it reaches the apex of its upward motion. For a drop volley, close the paddle angle just a little.

- **The ball always goes to the right or the left.** Make sure your body is turned all the way to the sideline on your backswing and when you hit the ball. The contact should occur when the ball is even with your front foot. Keep your wrist straight (don't let it flex) when the paddle hits the ball.

- **The ball always goes into the net.** With drop shots, try opening the paddle face slightly to pick the ball up a bit more or change your grip so that the paddle face is automatically a little more open. With drop volleys, you may be closing the face too much.

- **The ball doesn't travel far enough.** Start your swing sooner. Put a little more power into your swing, hitting up and through the ball. Make sure the paddle face is open. Carry the ball on your follow through, which should extend further than with a drive shot.

- **The wind carries or stops my shot.** This is more common with the drop shot than the drop volley. Take note of the direction and strength of the wind and alter the power and angle of your shot accordingly.

Midcourt Volley

This shot is very similar to the drop volley except that it is hit with power and is directed to the feet of your opponents. This shot is especially effective when you are at the non-volley line and your opponents are in the midcourt (sometimes referred to as "no man's land") — half way between the baseline and the non-volley zone. Keep the paddle face flat to slightly open. Angle the ball hard toward your opponent's feet where they will have a tough time returning it.

The potential problems with this shot are similar to those with the drop volley described earlier.

Dink

A dink is a soft shot, made with the paddle face open, and hit so that it *just clears the net* and drops into the non-volley zone. The dink is very similar to the drop shot except that it originates from within the non-volley zone or just behind the line.

The dink is used to keep your opponents from gaining the advantage or to take the advantage away from them when they are in good forecourt position.

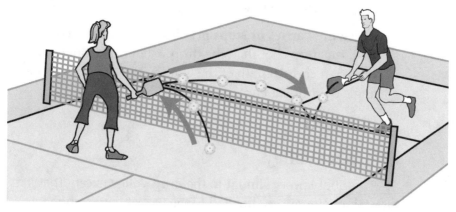

Figure 30. The dink is played off the bounce. The ball travels just over the net and lands in the non-volley zone.

A dink shot can be effective in catching your opponent off guard and it can change the rhythm of the game, allowing you to regain control of a rally that had you playing defense. Cross-court dinking is safer than dinking directly across from you because it provides a greater distance for the shot to travel.

The most common difficulty encountered with dinking is when your shot travels too high and your opponent smashes the ball back at you. If you hit the ball too low, however, the ball won't make it over the net, and the rally will be over. At least with a smash return from your opponent, you have a chance at returning it, so make sure the dink is high enough to travel over the net.

Dinking can continue for quite a long time. It has a slow pace and a rhythmic nature. *Don't be impatient.* Learning when and how to break out of the dink to hit a different shot is the key to winning the rally.

When you do break out of the dink, do it with power and speed to catch your opponent off guard.

Possible Problems with the Dink

- **The ball travels too far (doesn't land in the non-volley zone).** You may be putting too much power into your shot. Dinking requires finesse, not power. Don't take much of a preparatory motion or follow through. Just pop the ball over the net. Try angling your shot cross-court to give yourself more room to keep it in bounds.

- **The ball always goes into the net.** Open the paddle face slightly to pick the ball up a bit more or change your grip so that the paddle face is automatically a little more open. Try bending your knees more to get under the ball.

Half Volley

The half volley is often made as a defensive shot when someone has aimed the ball at your feet. However, it can also be used offensively as you move forward from the backcourt because the speed of the return may catch your opponent off guard. Hit ball immediately after the bounce. *Bend your knees to get down under the ball.*

The height of the shot is determined by the angle of your paddle face at the point of contact. What the angle of the face should be depends upon how close you are to the net. If you are close to the net, open the paddle face a little more to gain more height. If you are farther from the net, bring your paddle face more toward the flat position to keep the ball from traveling too high.

Start your backswing as you move into position and shift your weight to your back foot.

Bend your knees to get under the ball.

Continue to follow through. Your paddle should follow the trajectory of the ball.

From the ready position, turn toward the side where the ball will come.

Align your body parallel to the ball's flight. Swing "through the ball" as you step into the shot. Contact the ball in line with your front foot.

As your weight shifts to your forward foot, bring your back foot forward and move toward your next position.

Figure 31. The half volley.

Possible Problems with the Half Volley

- **Walking or running into the shot.** If you are moving forward when you start your forehand swing, the momentum of your forward movement will be added to the power of the shot, so you should hit the ball more softly to keep it in bounds.

- **The ball travels too far (out of bounds).** The face of your paddle may be open or you may be waiting too long to hit the ball. Keep the face of the paddle flat, and try to contact the ball very soon after the bounce, before it rises very far from the ground.

- **The ball always goes into the net.** Bend your knees more to get under the shot. Try opening the paddle face slightly to pick the ball up a bit more, or change your grip so that the paddle face is automatically a little more open.

Backhand and Forehand Sweeps

Sweep shots are sometimes necessary to return a ball that comes directly at you, especially during net volleys when play is very fast. You may not have time to return your paddle to the ready position, so the backhand or forehand sweep can help keep the ball in play.

Figure 32. The backhand sweep.

Your opponents may hit net volleys toward your chest (especially the backhand side of your chest) where they are hardest to return. During a net volley, instead of trying to return to the ready position between strokes, bring your paddle back about halfway between the backhand and ready position and prepare to make a backhand sweep. As the ball comes toward you, draw your paddle across your body, from your backhand to forehand side, either in a downward or upward motion (depending on the height of the ball), and keep the face toward the net throughout the stroke.

If you cannot get your paddle back into the modified ready/backhand position during a net volley, use the forehand sweep to return the ball. This shot draws your paddle across your body from the forehand side, keeping the paddle face toward the net throughout the stroke. These shots are difficult to master, so spend time practicing them.

Whatever the Shot, Keep Your Head Still

I've mentioned this when discussing the various types of shots, but it deserves a mention by itself. When you miss a shot, you may think you weren't watching the ball. That might not be the case. You might not have kept your head still.

When you hit a ball, your eyes instinctively follow the ball's path until the moment of contact (even if you can't really see the ball traveling that fast). Keeping your head still throughout the shot will help you maintain better balance. This is most important on shots close to the net, especially when you have to run up to reach the ball. It's very tempting to raise your head just before you contact the ball so you can watch the intended target. Typically this results in poor ball contact and a loss of accuracy.

Keep your head still through the entire swing and your shots will be more consistent and more accurate.

Get Ready for Each Shot

What happens if you don't make it up to the non-volley zone line and get caught in mid-court? It doesn't matter where you are on the court, whether you're still at the baseline or half-way up to the non-volley zone line: the moment your opponent hits the ball, assume the ready position. Don't just think, "Oh, I can just stop moving." Put your paddle up in front of you. Keep your weight on the balls of your feet and be ready to move, keeping your eye on the ball. Then, after you hit the ball, head for the non-volley zone as soon as it's safe to do so.

Spins

Adding spin to your strokes will make it more difficult for your opponent to return the ball. The type of spin to use depends on the shot you're trying to make, as well as the condition of the ball coming toward you.

The angle of your paddle face and the type of follow through will change the amount of spin applied to the ball. Experiment to see what works for you and practice these strokes to perfect their use during a game.

To apply *topspin*, move your paddle from low to high, bringing it up into the ball. Spins are one time when you should let your wrist turn at the end of the stroke and your elbow bend naturally on the follow through, following the curve of the spin applied to the ball. A ball with topspin spins forward in the direction it's traveling and drops more quickly than a normal ball with no spin. After the bounce, topspin causes the ball to rise quickly and then fall faster than normal (see Figure 34).

To apply *backspin* (also called *underspin*), move the paddle from high to low, bringing it down into the ball. Adding backspin is also known as slicing or chopping the ball. A ball with backspin turns away from the direction in which it's headed, and it generally rises slightly after it's hit, moving in a slower, more floating motion. After the ball hits the ground, it loses most of its forward momentum. The ball might bounce only a little or bounce in a more vertical direction, depending on the power put into the stroke, the angle of the paddle face, and the amount of spin given to the ball (see Figure 34).

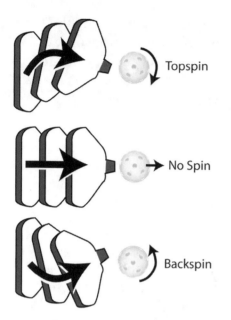

Topspin

Stroke the ball from low to high, causing the ball to spin in the direction of the shot. Some players also bring the face of the paddle up and over the ball during the follow through.

No Spin

Backspin

Stroke the ball from high to low. The ball spins away from the direction of the shot. Some players also bring the face of the paddle under the ball during the follow through.

Figure 33. Paddle positions to create different types of spin.

Applying *sidespin* isn't pictured in the illustrations here, but it is often combined with topspin or backspin (by moving the paddle up and to the side or down and to the side) and usually makes the ball harder to hit. To add sidespin, move your paddle from one side to the other as you contact the ball. Depending on the direction of the shot and the direction of the spin, sidespin will cause the ball to move toward or away from your opponent.

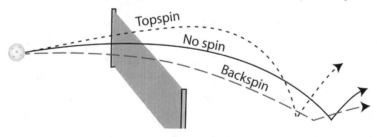

Figure 34. Different spins and how they affect the trajectory of the ball.

How do you deal with the spin your opponent uses against you? See "Returning Balls with Spin" on page 82.

Chapter 3

Court Positions and Footwork

The strongest court position in pickleball is close to the non-volley zone. This position allows you to return most of the balls that are hit to your court without having to travel as far. Conversely, the weakest position in pickleball is back near the baseline.

The diagram in Figure 35 shows the possible flight path of a ball hit by your opponent when playing singles.

Figure 35. Possible trajectory of your opponent's shot in singles.

Figure 36 shows the possible flight path of a ball hit by the opponent across from you when playing doubles. Despite the fact that you and your partner each have less far to move when playing together, being up close to the net reduces the distance you have to travel significantly.

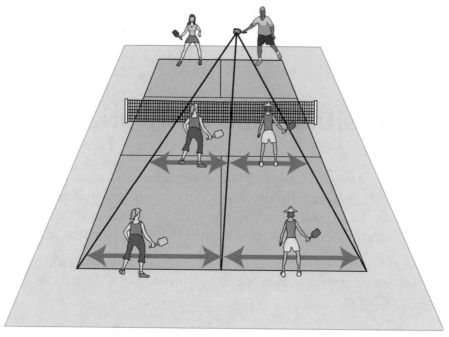

Figure 36. Possible trajectory of your opponent's shot in doubles.

Take a look at the lines with arrows. They show the distance you must cover if you're stationed in the forecourt or backcourt. When you are close to the non-volley zone, you must move a much smaller distance in order to reach a ball compared to when you are in the backcourt.

Your Position During a Serve

Both of the server's feet must be behind the baseline and at least one foot must be in contact with the ground or floor when the paddle contacts the ball.

Serving in Singles

Both the server and receiver should be positioned at the baselines. This allows both of you to accommodate the double-bounce rule.

Stand close to the centerline. This maximizes your ability to cover any extreme return your opponent might make.

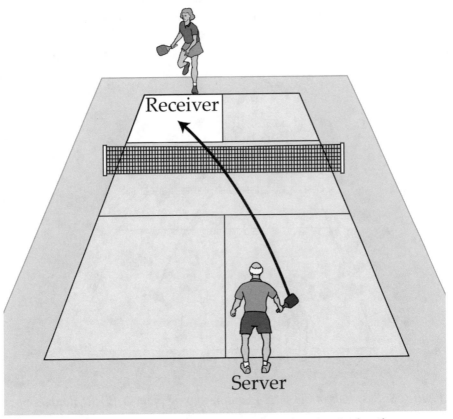

Figure 37. Positions of the server and receiver in singles play.

Serving in Doubles

In doubles, the two players on the serving team and the opponent receiving the ball usually stand at or behind their baselines. Why? To accommodate the double-bounce rule and enable all three of these players to retrieve a deep shot. The fourth player who is *not* receiving the serve should stand close to the non-volley zone since that is the strongest position. It is assumed that the receiving partner will move up to the non-volley zone as soon as possible after hitting the ball.

When playing doubles, you can stand close to the center-line or in the center of your half of the court, whichever you prefer. In fact, it can be a good idea to change your serving position frequently, varying the look and angle of the serve to keep your opponents off guard.

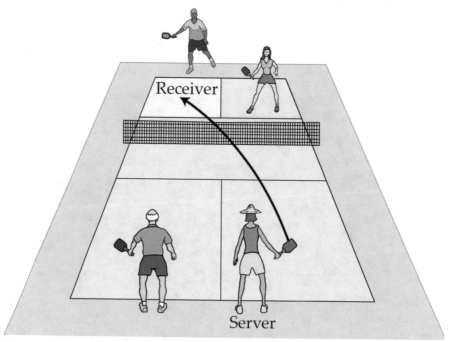

Figure 38. Positions of the serving and receiving players during doubles play.

The Art of Pickleball

Footwork and Moving into Position

Good footwork is often neglected by those learning a new sport, but that's the time to make sure it's right to avoid developing bad habits that later must be broken, something that is much harder to do.

Standing on the court flat footed denies you the ability to react quickly and robs you of precious split seconds when going for the ball. Stay on your toes. Keep your strides short and quick. Hurry back to the ready position after you make a stroke, and keep your feet moving. Dance a little!

Moving Toward a Shot and Around the Court

In pickleball, as in any court sport, good footwork is essential in helping you return some of the more difficult shots that come your way. A good opponent will try to put the ball where you are not. Besides anticipating the direction of the shot and being in the ready position so you can reach a shot more quickly, you need to be light on your feet, and your balance should be evenly distributed with your feet approximately shoulder-width apart.

Pivoting on the balls of your feet from the ready position will help you step quickly into either a forehand or backhand stroke. After pivoting, move whichever foot is closer to the net forward as you reach for the ball.

Learn to shuffle. When you need to move further than a single step, either sideways or backward, but not more than a couple of steps away, it's safest to shuffle or make a step-to-step motion (see Figure 39):

- Step out with the foot on the side to which you're moving.
- Bring your other foot up close to the first foot.
- Then step out with the first foot again.
- When you reach the correct court position, prepare and step into your swing as usual.

If you need to move further than just a couple of steps, pivot, run to the spot, and prepare for your shot.

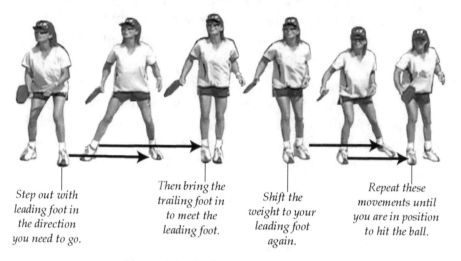

Step out with leading foot in the direction you need to go.

Then bring the trailing foot in to meet the leading foot.

Shift the weight to your leading foot again.

Repeat these movements until you are in position to hit the ball.

Figure 39. Shuffling across the court.

Good Footwork Helps Avoid Injury

One of the easiest ways to fall in pickleball is to run backward (without turning around) to get a ball that has been hit over your head. More falls in pickleball happen this way than any other. The next most common cause of injury comes from reaching for a shot that is beyond your balance point. Spills from both of these things can result in injuries to all portions of the body, depending what hits the ground, fence, or wall. I've seen players with casts or bruises and bumps as a result of "going for it" or running backward when they shouldn't have.

If you only have to move backward one or two steps, turn sideways, *toward the side where the ball will come,* and shuffle. (Turning toward the ball side will put you in position for the shot when you get there.) Do the same shuffle motion described above and then prepare for and take the shot.

Rush to the Non-Volley Zone

When you move forward from the baseline, keep your body facing forward. When you reach the desired position close to the non-volley zone, assume the ready position. All of this needs to be done *before* your opponent hits the ball.

Figure 40. Moving up to the non-volley zone.

Any time you can move close to the non-volley zone safely, do it. In doubles, it's best if both partners move in tandem, so if you can both move up safely, do so. If not, wait until both of you can. But what constitutes "safely"? When you are sure you'll have enough time to get to the non-volley line and not be caught in midcourt with a ball aimed at your feet or a drive headed to the backcourt that you won't be able to reach. Here are some examples:

- You return a drive shot that you know will go deep into your opponent's territory (and not be volleyed back).

- You lob a ball to the baseline.

- You're at the baseline and your opponent hits a ball that lands short of your position. (Move forward or diagonally into the ball and keep going.)

The main thing is to be on the watch for an opportunity to move up from the backcourt. When it presents itself, seize it and run forward.

Chapter 4

Warm-Ups and Fitness

⚠️ *Caution: The information provided in this chapter is intended for general reference purposes only. You should consult your doctor prior to starting any fitness or exercise program. The information presented here is not intended to address specific medical conditions and is not a substitute for professional medical advice or a medical exam. The advice of a trained fitness counselor may be valuable to tailor an exercise and fitness program to your individual needs.*

The smaller court size and the rules that help to equalize game play for both sexes and all ages have made it possible for many people who could not play other court sports to become quite good at pickleball. To take your game beyond your current level, however, you will need to get in shape physically. Concentrate on four things: flexibility, strength, endurance, and then practice.

Flexibility: Warming Up and *Then* Stretching

Flexibility helps prevent injury and allows you to reach shots that otherwise might get by you. Some players think flexibility means getting to the court, doing a few stretches, and then starting a game. Stretching should **not** be done without raising the body temperature slightly (about 3 degrees) above normal. To do this, walk briskly, run in place, or do any aerobic activity that will get you warmed up. Only then should you stretch your muscles or start playing pickleball.

Warming up does more than just loosen stiff muscles: done properly, it improves performance. An improper warm-up, or no warm-up at all, can increase your risk of injury from athletic activities.

The goals of a warm-up are improved coordination, improved elasticity and contractibility of muscles, and greater efficiency of your respiratory and cardiovascular systems. *Active or isometric stretches should not be part of your warm-up* because the stretched muscles may to be too tired to perform well during the actual athletic activity.

1. Warming Up

Good, general warm-up activity consists of joint rotations followed by aerobic activity. Spend 10 to 15 minutes warming up.

Begin with **joint-rotations** from your toes up or your neck down. Such rotations facilitate joint motion by lubricating the joint with fluid, permitting it to function more easily. Perform slow, circular movements, both clockwise and counterclockwise, until each joint seems to move smoothly.

After joint rotations, begin **aerobic activity** such as jogging or jumping rope for approximately five minutes (or until you begin to sweat). This raises your core body temperature and gets your blood pumping. Increased blood flow in the muscles improves muscle performance and flexibility and reduces the possibility of injury.

After you are warmed up, begin static stretching.

2. Static Stretching

Once the general warm-up has been completed, the muscles are warmer and more elastic. Immediately following your general warm-up, start slow, relaxed, **static stretching.** Begin with your back, followed by your upper body, and then your lower body.

Static stretching involves holding a position: stretch only to the farthest point and hold the stretch for a few seconds. **Do not bounce**—bouncing or jerking can damage your muscles and joints. Instead, stretch until resistance is felt, hold it there for about 3 seconds, then release. (It used to be common to hold stretches for up to 30 seconds or more. Recent research indicates that this can also be damaging to muscles, so it is recommended that you keep your holding time very short—only a few seconds.)

If you don't have time to stretch all these muscles before a workout, at least stretch all the muscles that will be used the most when you play.

Static stretches should be performed *before* dynamic stretches. Performing static stretches first helps reduce the risk of injury (yes, even stretching can be tough on your body, so be careful).

3. Dynamic Stretching

Once you have performed the static stretches, do some light **dynamic stretching**: *controlled* leg and arm movements that take you carefully to the limits of your range of motion (and not beyond). Do not work your muscles to the point of fatigue. Remember: this is just a warm-up. The real workout comes later when you play.

Sport-specific stretching. The last part of your warm-up could include "watered-down" versions of movements used in pickleball. Such sport-specific activity improves coordination, balance, strength, and response time, and hopefully will reduce the risk of injury.

Strength

You may be shaking your head, saying, "Pickleball doesn't require strength—that's part of what makes it so enjoyable and allows everyone to play." You're right. However, a certain amount of muscle strength *is* required in order to prevent injury that otherwise might claim your elbows, shoulders, knees, and more. Joint injury in pickleball is common but can be avoided through the proper conditioning. Start a regimen of weight training that will help strengthen your joints and muscles. Do it two to three times per week—not on consecutive days.

It's best to train the large muscle groups first. Working on your thighs, chest, abdomen, and back will consume the majority of your energy, so it's best to work on these when you're strongest. After that, exercise the smaller muscles (calves, biceps, triceps, and forearms). They don't require as much energy to train.

- Start slowly and increase as you become stronger. If you are new to strength training, for the first two to three weeks, start with one set of 12 repetitions per muscle group. A good rule of thumb for starting weight, if you are in good health, is one that will allow you to do 8 to 12 repetitions. If you can't do at least 8 repetitions, the weight is too heavy. If you can do more than 12 repetitions easily, the weight is too light. Try to learn at least two exercises for each major muscle group, including your back, chest, shoulders, arms, legs, and abdomen.

- Rest for 30 to 60 seconds between sets of exercises.

- When you are able, add another set of each exercise so that you perform two sets of 12 repetitions each.

- After you can successfully complete two sets of 12 repetitions for each exercise, gradually increase the weight. Adding weight, not repetitions, will increase your capability and add muscle.

Aerobic Endurance

Endurance is what will keep you going through an entire match, no matter how much your opponent keeps you running. Sometimes you may have to play *many* points before a winner is determined. If you are in good shape and you have endurance, you'll be able to keep going, returning difficult shots, and won't be worn out before the match is over.

The best way to increase your endurance is to engage in a *rhythmic* aerobic activity, such as walking, running, cycling, or swimming. To gauge whether you are doing the right amount of aerobic exercise, talk out loud. You should be able to carry on a breathy conversation while working out. If you can't talk at all, your routine is too difficult. If you can speak more than about ten words at a time without needing a breath, increase your workout.

Do your aerobic exercise at least three times a week for 20 to 30 minutes each time.

Tennis Elbow

Tennis elbow (lateral epicondylitis) is a degenerative condition of the muscles and tendons on the outside of the elbow. Typically, it is the result of overuse or repetitive stress, and can occur after any repetitive motion of the hand and/or arm. Usually, tennis elbow results in pain or stiffness in movements of the elbow and sometimes the hand and often produces forearm muscle tightness.

Some people seem to be naturally more prone to developing joint and muscle problems when playing paddle or racquet sports. Strengthening your muscles *before* developing tennis elbow is the best course of action. If you begin developing symptoms, don't ignore them. Many players (and I am included in this group) have been guilty of not taking tennis elbow seriously and continuing to play despite pain or other symptoms. It can become a chronic, lingering problem if not cared for properly.

Consider changing your equipment or how you use it: get a lighter paddle, add tape to your grip to make it larger, or change the way you hold the paddle. Have someone watch you swing and make sure you're doing it properly. Sometimes a very simple change will bring instant results.

There are also strengthening and flexibility exercises you can do that will help reduce the pain and will encourage healing, and there are bands or braces you can wear that will help to ease the symptoms. Cold packs can be helpful, too. Ask your doctor or other medical professional to explain what you can do to help alleviate the problem. There are a number of web sites that contain good information. The references listed for this book contain one that seemed particularly good.

Chapter 5

Strategies and Tactics

Pickleball is fun to play, even when you are new to the sport. As you play more and your competence rises, however, you may begin thinking about how you could win more often. It's still fun to play, even if you don't win. However, as others have pointed out before, if it didn't matter whether you win or lose, you wouldn't keep score.

It's more fun to win. This chapter presents information designed to help you win more often. But either way, have fun!

At the end of this chapter are diagrams showing many different player positions on the pickleball court. When you finish the chapter, study these diagrams and decide what kind of shot(s) you would make in each instance. After each diagram is a page showing a list of answers, in order of recommendation by those I interviewed, and why they are suggested.

You may have noticed already that some of the information in this book is contradictory. For example, I've pointed out often that you should move up to the non-volley zone as soon as possible; there is also a statement suggesting you stay back if you think the opponents will smash the ball at you. Both statements are true. Because situations and players differ, it's up to you to determine the *best* course of action since more than one is usually "right." The circumstances surrounding the shot help you to know what to do.

Beware of taking advice (even the information presented in this book) without making sure that it works for you. Tips that work well for pros may not be suitable for novice players, for example. Try new things during practice so you'll be ready with new ammunition when you encounter better players or reach the tournament.

One more thing: the tactics described here assume you are not playing in a situation where you are trying to be "nice" to your opponent. If you're playing with friends, for example, you probably don't want to smash the ball back into their bodies or continually take advantage of their weaknesses—two things that are described below. Keep in mind that the hints given in this book are designed to help you win. You may want to tailor their application to your particular situation.

General Tactics and Strategies

Your main tactical goals are to:

- Keep the ball in play by playing the best (and safest) shots for the given situation,

- Keep your opponent on the run,

- Take advantage of your opponent's weaknesses.

The rest of this chapter describes strategies for achieving these goals.

Make a Game Plan

As with any sport, much of the game of pickleball is mental. Whether you win or lose often depends on your reactions as the game goes along, whether you feel good about your playing or not, and so on. Concentrating on the score, especially if it's not going well, often only makes you play worse, not better.

Most athletes use techniques to rid themselves of negative thoughts and remain calm. One of the simplest techniques is to concentrate on something else, such as the ball. But another way that may prove useful for you is to develop a personal game plan before heading to the court.

This can be anything you wish, but it should be specific and short. For example, I sometimes make a plan to concentrate on staying ready for the next shot—on being light on my feet—and I continue chanting that to myself, in my mind, as the game goes along. This frees me from worrying about the score or whether or not I'm playing as well as I might. My plan might also include watching for weaknesses in my opponent's game that I hadn't known ahead of time, as well as learning his strengths so I might avoid giving him points. A plan might be as simple as returning every shot or concentrating on watching the ball.

When you're playing doubles, begin planning together well before the game begins, off the court. Your strategy might include what you know of your opponents' strengths and weaknesses. Discuss the kinds of shots you could use against each opponent, and where the best placement for those shots might be. You might also talk about your own strengths and how to minimize your weaknesses. Plan strategies to deal with a poor backhand, for example, or what to do if both of you call a shot.

Decide which of you will cover centerline returns and who will cover lobs. Discuss what vocal signals you will use. Talk over your plans for switching courts as needed and the poaching methods you will use, if any. If you plan to shadow each other, make that known, or, if you will play fore- or backcourt positions, make that clear.

In short, think about all the things that occur during a game and plan how you'll handle each one. Take time to think about how you'll handle the mental game as well, and you'll be well on your way to game success.

Improve Your Serve

- **Put your serve into the correct service court.** I cannot stress enough the importance of doing this. Pickleball is different from tennis in this regard. You don't get a second try, and most serves, no matter how good they might be, are returned. Don't try to "ace" the serve. Your serve can be slow, high, or otherwise less than stellar, but, if it lands in the service court, you are that much closer to making a point. If you miss the service court, your attempt at the point is lost. So read the suggestions below and try them—but remember: get the serve into the service court.

- **Call the score *just before* you serve**—not while you're serving and not too far ahead of the serve. Call the score—then leave a few seconds for any questions or corrections before starting the serve. Doing this alerts all the players that you are preparing to serve the ball. Calling the score while you serve is very distracting to you and your opponents and is considered to be poor etiquette on the court. You'll find that anything occurring while you serve will cause you to serve out of bounds, into the net, or otherwise to serve poorly.

- **Vary your serve.** If you served deep before, try a short serve to throw your opponents off guard.

- **Try deep serves to the baseline.** Players can sometimes be caught "creeping" into the court area and, because they must play the ball off a bounce, they'll have trouble doing so if they are too close.

- **Serve to your opponent's backhand.** Most players are weaker on the backhand side, and their reach isn't as long, so this is typically a good strategy.

- **Serve low and fast** since these serves are generally harder to return than high, slow ones.

Improve Your Returns to Stay on the Offense

- **Watch how your opponent hits the ball.** Pay attention to the angle of his paddle, in particular. This may alert you to any spin he may have applied, clueing you where the ball may be aimed. Also, the speed of his stroke may indicate that you need to change your court position. Quick exchanges at the non-volley zone make this kind of watchfulness crucial. Speed also makes it easier to make errors, especially by hitting balls too hard, causing them to fly out of bounds. Anticipating a ball that has been hit hard might give you time to step aside, letting the ball fly past you out of bounds.

- **If your opponents are at the baseline, keep them there and on the defense** by hitting drives deep at their feet unless you have a good overhead smash shot. This will keep your opponents back and prevent them from gaining good position at the non-volley zone. If you and your partner are back as well, you should start moving immediately so that you will gain good court position at the non-volley zone before your opponent hits the ball.

- **Don't pop a shot up to the "in-between" area that gives your opponent an opportunity for a smash.** Return shots often fail because they are not high enough or deep enough to be good lobs or not low enough to be difficult for your opponent to return. The pop up shot allows your opponent to smash the ball back at you, typically right into your body or to your feet, where it is difficult for you to return it.

- **When receiving a serve, try to hit a deep return and then move forward to join your partner at the net volley position.** From there, you can hit overhead smashes and dink shots, while the serving team, still on the defensive, must use passing or drive shots, overhead lobs, and drop shots into the non-volley zone, hoping to cause you to fault and giving them time to gain better court position.

- Many players have adopted a strategy that seems to work quite well. I call it the **"third shot drop shot."** When you are serving, send the ball deep into your opponent's court. They will generally return it deeply since this gives them time to get up to the non-volley zone line. Make your next shot a drop shot that lands just over the net in the non-volley zone. Since your opponents are already there, this shot gains them nothing. Now, however, you also have time to move up to the non-volley zone line, and there is another benefit to this strategy: it puts the game into soft mode and stops your opponents (for a while at least) from hitting hard, deep shots that can be tough to return. This strategy calls for you and your partner to be good at the soft game, able to dink back and forth patiently until one of you has the opportunity to make a put-away shot and win the rally.

- **Don't always hit the ball back down the center.** When playing against a doubles team for the first time, hit your first return down the line, if possible, rather than back toward the server. Most opponents expect you to return the serve down the center since that is considered the practical shot. If your line drive wins the rally, or if you just miss getting the ball in, the server's partner will probably not favor the center again, opening it up for you. Otherwise, angle the ball toward the server's sideline so that he has to stretch to reach it. The point is that you shouldn't return everything up the middle — your opponents find those shots easier to return. Make them uncertain about where to play from the beginning of the game.

- Pat Kane says **it's best to hit the ball where your opponent is not.** He points out that the better players are often able to retrieve balls hit at their feet or directly at them, so he feels the best shots are made to an open area of the court.

- Being on the offense means you have time to hit the ball where and how you wish, making your opponent react as best he can — so he is playing on the defensive and will not likely be able to put you on the defensive during the rally. **The more times during a rally that you are in control, the more likely you are to win that rally.** This is why it is important that you *hit shots that have a purpose* instead of simply returning the ball and hoping your opponent will hit it out or into the net. Continue applying pressure to your opponent in order to make his returns more difficult.

- If your opponent is in the midcourt area, **return the ball hard and fast to his feet or directly at him,** depending on how far he is from the non-volley line. A fast return aimed at your opponent's body will be very difficult for him to return.

- **If your opponents send you a high ball, always smash it back.** This works best when you are closer to the net, but it can also be done effectively from the mid- or backcourt areas. Never pass up an opportunity for a smash.

- **If you need to hit a low ball, try a dink, drop shot, or lob.** What to do depends on where you are on the court. If you're close to the non-volley zone line, dink the ball. From further back, try a drop shot that flies low and lands just over the net. If you can't do either of those, lob the ball high, over your opponent's head near the baseline.

- **Hit overhead shots in the air** rather than letting them bounce. Exceptions to this are:

  - If the ball will bounce in the non-volley zone and bounce high enough that you can smash it back.

  - If you are at the baseline and your return might fall short or might not have the power to be a good smash.

  - If you are at the baseline and the ball might go out.

When and How to Make Dink Shots

- **If you can't make a good offensive shot, a dink shot may be a good alternative,** especially if your opponents are already in strong forecourt position. However, if one or both of your opponents are in the backcourt, especially if they are good at dinking, refrain from trying the dink, since this will only cause them to rush up to the net to play the ball. If your opponents are *not* good at dinking or you don't think they will be able to get to the ball from the backcourt, a dink can be a good play.

- **The key to good dinking is patience.** You must continue to dink until a proper moment appears to execute a different, offensive shot. The best dink shots arc just over the net, landing close to the net on the other side. In doubles, it can be wise to send the dink cross-court because the ball can travel further, reducing the risk that your ball will travel out of the non-volley zone, allowing your opponent to volley the ball back to you. Don't send the dink shot out of bound, though. Try to maneuver your opponents around the court until one of them makes a mistake, either hitting the ball into the net or high enough that you can make an offensive shot. When this occurs, volley the ball back quickly.

- **While dinking, it helps to let the ball travel higher before hitting it.** Some people say you should hit the ball closer to the ground, citing that its faster motion assists in getting the ball over the net. However, the dink is a soft shot and doesn't require much energy. Let the ball approach the top of its arc. At that point, you have the option of either hitting another dink or making a fast slap shot if it bounces high enough.

- Dink shots have no real speed behind them, so **breaking out of dinking requires that you add a little more energy to the hard swing** you would normally make (when it's time).

- **Don't back up to play the dink off the bounce when it could be taken in the air.** Dinking is done for two reasons: to change the pace of the game and to keep the ball in play until you can end the rally with a put-away shot. When you're given the opportunity to make the put away, seize it.

When and How to Make Lob Shots

- Lobs are most often made as defensive shots. While they can be used offensively, do not use an offensive lob if you have a different offensive shot available instead.

- **A good service return is the soft, floating lob that lands in the backcourt** because it keeps the serving team there and allows you to get to the non-volley line. This shot is not dangerous on a service return since your opponent must let the ball bounce and cannot return the lob using an overhead smash.

- **The deep, soft lob is one of the easiest shots to make.** Take care when positioning the shot. If the lob is too long, you'll lose the rally when it lands out of bounds; if it's too short, your opponent will likely return an overhead smash.

- **A lob is effective when both of your opponents are at the non-volley line** and expect a drive return or dink shot. Sending a high, deep lob will force your opponents back to the baseline and may cause them to fault or make a poor return. Don't use the lob too often or you'll lose the element of surprise that makes this shot work well.

- **Use a lob when you need to move back into position at the non-volley line.** This shot is useful when one partner has moved out of position to retrieve a shot or when both of you are in the backcourt.

- **When your opponent hits a lob or high return, look to see if you can smash it back.** If possible, direct the slam/smash to the opponent who is closest to the net and who will have the least amount of time to react. Sending the smash to your opponent's feet makes it hardest for him to return.

- **Anticipate your opponent's lob shot.** If your partner moves to the net to retrieve a dink shot, your opponent may try a lob shot into the open court behind your partner. Call your partner off the shot and cover it for him.

- **Whenever possible, return the lob shot as a volley, before it has a chance to bounce.** Letting the lob bounce gives your opponents time to gain position at the net (which is one of the reasons they will use the lob in the first place). Sometimes you must let a lob bounce (when you lose sight of it in the sun, when you must run back to hit it, or when you aren't sure if it will land out of bounds and let it bounce to be sure). Any other time, volley the lob with an overhead smash, if possible.

- **Try to hit the lob over your opponent's backhand side.** A high backhand shot is one of the most difficult shots for anyone to hit.

- **If you don't execute the lob well,** and you know it will land short, **move back,** anticipating the smash your opponents will make.

Returning Balls with Spin

Before getting to the specific tips, I need to discuss conflicting thoughts about this subject. Some of the players I interviewed insist that you should not add spin to a spinning ball. Instead, they say you should contact it flat, putting no spin of your own onto it. Others say doing this usually puts the ball into the net. Their feeling is that you should either use a counterspin (putting your own topspin on a ball with topspin, for example) or add an additional amount of the same spin to the ball, making it that much harder for your opponent to return.

I suggest you decide which is best for your particular style and level of play. If you find that your technique causes you to return spinning balls into the net or out of bounds, try doing it the other way.

- Get to the non-volley zone quickly so you can **hit spinning balls before they bounce.** Balls with underspin and sidespin tend to remain in the air for a long time and are volleyed easily.

- **If you can't volley a spinning ball, move into the ball and hit it about waist height or just below.** Don't let the ball drop too low, as it becomes more difficult to hit.

- **Watch closely as your opponent gets ready and hits the ball.** Notice the angle of each spin, and log it away for future reference, since the next one will probably be very similar to the first. After a few of these, you'll be able to recognize which spin he's using and prepare for it. When you see him striking the ball from above (high to low), you know a backspin is coming. When his paddle starts below the ball on the backswing and hits it from low to high, prepare for a topspin. If he pulls his paddle across his body, most likely he's putting sidespin on the ball.

Position Yourself on the Court

- **Remain behind the baseline after the serve** to be ready for a deep return without having to move backward. A good opponent will watch for you to stand too close and send a hard drive to your feet at the baseline—a shot that's very hard to return.

- **Move up to the non-volley zone as soon as it's safe to do so.** The team that gains this position first is in the strongest position to win the rally. Your feet should be between six inches and a foot behind the non-volley line. Give yourself enough room to pivot and step into a swing as you hit the ball without touching the non-volley line. During a serve, the non-receiving player should remain close to the non-volley line, and the receiving player should move in as soon as possible.

  When is it safe? When you believe you'll have time to get there and not get caught in midcourt. One example is when you hit a deep drive. As soon as you realize your opponent will either remain near or move to his baseline to hit the ball, run up to your non-volley line.

  Novice players hate moving up to the non-volley zone. Often they end up in midcourt, halfway between the baseline and the non-volley zone. This position is called "no-man's land" for a reason—it's actually worse there than staying in the backcourt, since a savvy opponent will smash the ball at your feet or legs. If you find that you just can't get to the net, don't linger in midcourt. Stay back near the baseline until you are comfortable moving up quickly to the non-volley zone.

- **If you or your partner are at the baseline and accidentally send the ball high to an opponent at the non-volley zone, stay where you are.** There is a good likelihood that your opponent will smash the ball back to one of you, and you'll need room to get behind the smash to return it. Only if your shot clears the opponent at the net or goes deep into the opponents' court should you move up.

- **Stay in motion.** One of the laws of physics states that an object in motion tends to stay in motion, and an object at rest tends to stay at rest. In pickleball, this law applies to *you* as well as to the ball. If you wait for the ball with both feet flat on the court, it will be harder for you to reach a ball that is hit far from you than if you are moving your weight from one foot to the other.

- **Turn your body** (not just your head or eyes) **to face the opponent who is hitting the ball.** You will then be in the best position to return whatever shot comes your way.

- **Don't drop your guard.** Keep your paddle in the ready position, even when you are *sure* the ball will not be returned. Even the best pickleball shots can be returned by a player having good defensive strategies, so concentrate and be ready for a return.

- **Volley as many balls as you can.** To do this effectively, you must be at the non-volley line. When you can't volley, fast, low shots are usually the best.

- When you are in position at the non-volley line, you are on the offense since you can volley most effectively from this position. **When you're in the backcourt, you're playing defense, and you should look for every opportunity to move forward safely and assume the offense.**

- **Stay close to the center line of the court** (or your half of the court when playing doubles) or return to the center if you move out to retrieve a shot. Don't stand in the spot where you hit the ball to see what will happen next. Moving back to the center gives you the best position to return any shot that comes to you.

Limit Your Faults

In his book about pickleball, Mark Friedenberg says, "limiting your errors is the most important strategy in this book." He lists some very interesting statistics:

"Three of every four rallies (75 percent) are won (or lost) because of errors... One of every four rallies (25 percent) are actually earned or won by a good shot... Three out of every four errors (75 percent) are made at the baseline by hitting the ball into the net or out of bounds."[7]

Here are some ways to help avoid faults during the game.

- If you do nothing else to improve your pickleball game, try to do this: **keep the ball in play.** Always try to hit the ball, barring a shot that would cause you injury, since that will at least give you a chance to win a rally. If you don't keep the ball in play, you can't win. It's that simple.

- **Don't put the ball into the net.** Often it's the fast return or the hard smash that ends up there. Whenever possible, take time enough *(be patient)* to ensure that your shot will go over the net. Most players hit their shots too low. This is especially true when you don't have time to prepare a drive stroke properly and it doesn't fly high enough. If you're playing singles, your balls can fly a little higher since your opponent has no partner who is likely to smash a ball back from the non-volley zone.

- **Don't send the ball out of bounds.** This sounds simple enough, but it is why people will tell you to send most of your shots down the center of the court. It's safer there, with less chance that you'll make a fault. Another good strategy is to hit the ball deep and moderately crosscourt. Hitting the ball within the middle 2/3 of the court makes your shot less likely to go wide, and the ball travels over the lower part of

---

7. Friedenberg, Mark, *The Official Pickleball Handbook* (Tacoma, WA: PB Master, 1999), 29.

the net. You are also hitting more safely into a longer, diagonal court. Typically, aiming about three feet inside your opponent's baseline will prevent the ball from landing out of bounds but will be deep enough to give you time to react to your opponent's next shot.

- **Don't try a risky shot when a safe one would do equally well.** In your zeal to be a "good" player, you may feel that you'll only be good if you can place your ball into an unreachable corner or smash a ball perfectly. While these shots are fine, they are not the "bread and butter" of pickleball, and many games are won without them. What wins in pickleball? Getting the ball back over the net, hopefully in a way that makes it harder for your opponent to hit, but at least getting it there. After that, there's the hope that your opponents will make a mistake and cause a fault. If not, you have another chance to make a shot they may not be able to return.

- **When you are near the non-volley zone, pay attention to the location of your feet.** Stepping on the line or into the non-volley zone while volleying is a fault.

Target Your Opponents' Weaknesses

- **If you discover something that works** well against your opponents (e.g., hitting to a weak backhand), **keep doing it.**

- If one of your opponents is weaker than the other, **return shots to the weaker player.**

- **The backhand is usually weaker than the forehand for most players.** If you don't know your opponents, try aiming your shot to their backhand side until you know what their strengths are.

- **Notice unprotected areas of the court and put the ball there.** This is especially true when playing doubles: keep an eye out for gaps in your opponents' positions that provide a place for a winning shot.

- If one opponent is left-handed and one right-handed, there will be times when both of their backhands will be toward center court. When you see this occur, try a hard, passing shot down the middle when they're at the net or a hard line drive down the middle when they're in the backcourt.

- **In doubles play, passing shots or line drives down the middle of the court are generally good** for two reasons: there may be confusion regarding which player should return the shot, and you're more likely to keep the ball in bounds.

- **Sending a passing shot by a player rushing the net can cause him to return it while he's off balance** or without the ability to prepare properly. Be careful when sending a passing shot or line drive down the outside of the court, since these shots can easily land out of bounds, and your chances of putting the ball into the net or hitting the ball out of the court are greater. Still, it's good to try this shot once in a while for the sake of variety that keeps your opponents guessing what you'll do next.

- **Keep your opponent moving and on the defensive.** In pickleball, every extra step your opponent must take is to your advantage.

- **If you are generally better than your opponents, don't change your usual game.** If they are better than you are, make them do things they wouldn't usually do. Keep them running, send them after difficult shots, etc.

- **If your opponents are doing better than you are, call a time out.** Breaking the rhythm of the game stops their streak, and gives you time to relax, talk over what to do, smile, joke, and otherwise break the tension. It's amazing how many times this works.

Keep Your Opponent Guessing

I've mentioned this before, but let's look at it in depth. It's best to vary any strategy with others that keep your opponents off guard. Don't always play the same way. Using a large repertoire of shots limits your opponents' ability to anticipate your next move.

Besides just varying your serve, your return, or other standard shots, one method I've seen that often works is to look in one direction and hit the ball somewhere else. Again, don't do it repeatedly. This kind of play is most effective when your opponent doesn't expect it.

Similarly, hitting a very soft shot when your opponents are prepared for a smash return can catch them off guard. This is especially true when they are in the back court and will have trouble getting up to the net in time to hit the ball. It's most effective to angle the soft shot toward the outside of the court if this softer shot allows you to make it with accuracy.

Think One Step Ahead

You've probably watched a great game of pool or billiards and noticed that a great player doesn't just hit *this shot*—he plans and prepares for the *next shot* at the same time.

In the same way, you need to think ahead to what your opponent might do if you make a certain play. You should also think about the consequences of wind or sun if you're playing outdoors. If you lob, for example, will the wind carry the ball right or left and, if so, should you angle your shot differently? If you hit a hard drive, where will your opponent hit it back and how will you return that shot?

You can also try to set up shots so you and your partner work together. Hitting a short shot, for example, that causes your opponent to run in to get the ball, often means he'll send his return high, allowing you or your partner to smash it back and win the rally.

Positional Strategies

The following pages ask you to analyze what the best shot(s) might be when playing doubles, depending on the players' positions on the court. List what you think the best options might be and why you think so. Then compare your ideas to the answers (a consensus of my thoughts and those of the people I interviewed). In this way, I hope you'll gain a better understanding of positional tactics and why one shot might be better than another in a certain situation.

The positions shown assume that the double-bounce has already occurred. In all the positions that follow, "your" position is noted with a circle around the player on the closest court.

First a note about the diagrams. I've diagrammed every possible position for doubles players on the court. Not all of them are likely to occur, at least not in more advanced play. Bill Booth, who brought pickleball to Sun City Grand in Arizona, said it succinctly when looking at position one on the next page: "What are my opponents doing back there? They have hit an excellent approach shot by hitting it deep into the backcourt. They should have followed their shot in and not stayed back to admire it." He's correct, of course, but I have included it just because it is a *possible* position, and thinking about your answers in that situation encourages deeper knowledge of strategies and tactics in returning a shot.

The answers are listed in order of preference, although sometimes it was hard to rate one shot as better than another. Which is best sometimes depends on the players and their abilities, since some shots require more expertise than others. Other times, it depends on how the ball comes to you: is it a lob, or a low, hard shot? You'll have to think about these possibilities when describing your answers and when you read the listed choices.

Position 1

Your opponents are both at the baseline.
The ball comes fast and deep to you.
What shots might you make and why?

_____

_____

_____

_____

_____

Position 1: Answers

1. Hit a hard, deep drive to your opponent's feet or to center court to create confusion over which opponent will return it. This is the best and safest shot you can make. A deep drive should keep your opponents back, preventing them from gaining good position at the non-volley zone.

2. Try a drop shot so that the ball lands just behind the net in the non-volley zone. This is a difficult shot to execute, and is not as good as the drive in this instance because it invites your opponents to come up to the net.

    If your shot goes as you want it to, start moving up immediately after executing the shot so that you will gain good court position at the non-volley zone *before your opponent hits the ball.* If the shot doesn't do what you wanted it to, remain where you are until you're sure it's safe to move up.

The Art of Pickleball

Position 2

Your opponents are split, with one at the baseline
and one at the non-volley zone, and you and your partner
are in the backcourt. The ball comes deep to you.
What shots might you make and why?

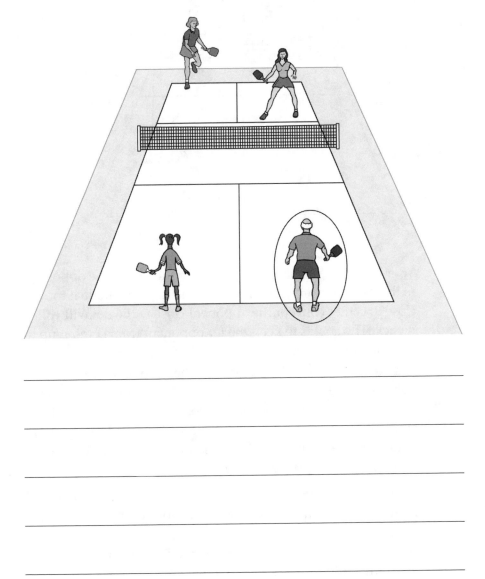

_____

_____

_____

_____

_____

Position 2: Answers

1. Your best shot is a hard, deep drive to the feet of the opponent in the backcourt to keep him where he is. Don't angle it too close to center court or the opponent close to the net will volley it back. The goal is to keep the far opponent from coming up to the non-volley zone and gaining better position.

2. Less good but possible is a lob over the head of the closer opponent. Again, the goal is to keep or send your opponents away from the non-volley zone, but the lob has a tendency to fall short, allowing a smash return, or to go long, ending up out of bounds. Be ready for the far opponent to field the return. If this occurs, the two opponents might switch sides.

   If your shot goes as you want it to, start moving up immediately after executing the shot so that you will gain good court position at the non-volley zone *before your opponent hits the ball.* If the shot doesn't do what you wanted it to, remain where you are until you're sure it's safe to move up.

Position 3

Your opponents are both at the non-volley zone.
You and your partner are both in the backcourt.
The ball comes deep to you.
What shots might you make and why?

_____

_____

_____

_____

_____

_____

Position 3: Answers

1. Hit a drop shot into the non-volley zone. This shot is more difficult to make than the lob (later), but it gives you and your partner time to gain the net and reduces the risk that your opponents will smash the return back.

2. A hard, passing shot down the sideline is the shot with the most risk, but it can be effective, especially if your opponent expects something else.

3. Less good but possible is a lob over either opponent's head. You can send it to center court, hoping some confusion may arise as to which one will go for the shot, or to the backhand of the player outside (more risky). Again, the goal is to send your opponents away from the non-volley zone, but the lob has a tendency to fall short, allowing a smash return, or to go long, ending up out of bounds.

If your shot goes as you want it to, start moving up immediately after executing the shot so that you will gain good court position at the non-volley zone *before your opponent hits the ball.* If the shot doesn't do what you wanted it to, remain where you are until you're sure it's safe to move up.

Position 4

Your opponents are both at the baseline.
The ball comes to you at the non-volley zone.
Your partner is still in the backcourt.
What shots might you make and why?

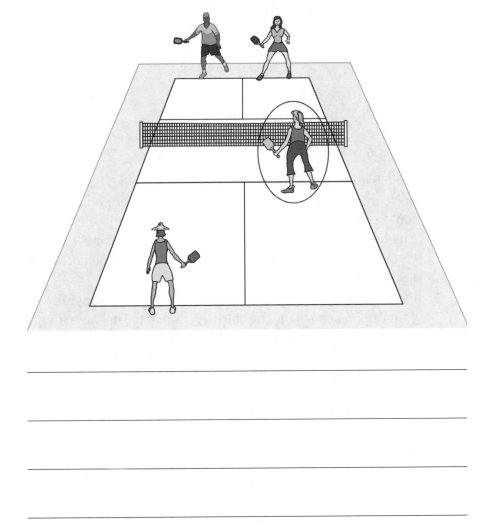

_____

_____

_____

_____

_____

Position 4: Answers

1. If the ball coming to you is high enough, smash it back to an open area on the court (trying for a shot that your opponents can't return) or toward the feet of either opponent. If the ball isn't high, hit a drive in the same directions. Remember that you have a lot of angles and room to play when you are at the net and your opponents are still in the backcourt.

2. Dink the ball (cross-court gives you more room). Hopefully your opponents will not be able to get up to the net fast enough to reach it. If you can start the dink with a drop volley, it is even more likely to be successful. If you let the ball bounce first, your opponents will have more time to get to the line and your dink will be less surprising. The drawbacks to the dink shot are that it does bring your opponents to the non-volley zone, and your partner still needs time to get to the non-volley zone, too.

    If your shot goes as planned, your partner should start moving up immediately to gain good court position at the non-volley zone *before your opponent hits the ball*. If the shot doesn't do what you wished, be prepared to move back (and your partner should stay where he is) to get the return.

Position 5

Your opponents are split, with one at the
non-volley zone and the other at the baseline.
Your partner is still in the backcourt.
The ball comes to you at the non-volley zone.
What shots might you make and why?

_____

_____

_____

_____

Position 5: Answers

1. If the ball is high enough, smash it back near the feet of the close opponent.
2. If the ball isn't high enough to smash, hit a hard shot to the feet of the far opponent. This will give your partner time to come in to the non-volley line.
3. Dink the ball wide into the open area in front of the far opponent, hoping that he may not be able to get to the ball in time.

    If your shot goes as planned, your partner should start moving up immediately to gain good court position at the non-volley zone *before your opponent hits the ball.* If the shot doesn't do what you wished, be prepared to move back (and your partner should stay where he is) to get the return.

Position 6

Your opponents are both at the non-volley zone.
Your partner is still at the baseline.
The ball comes to you at the non-volley zone.
What shots might you make and why?

Position 6: Answers

1. If the ball coming to you is high enough, smash it back to the feet of either opponent.

2. Dink the ball (cross-court gives you the most room). Then wait for your opponents to return a shot that's just a little too high or too long and make a fast, hard shot they won't expect or be able to return. Dinking can be dangerous, however, if you don't think your partner can join you at the non-volley line soon enough.

3. Lob the ball over either opponent's head. You can send it to center court, hoping some confusion may arise as to which one will go for the shot, or to the backhand of the player outside (more risky). Again, the goal is to send your opponents away from the non-volley zone, and the lob gives your partner the most time to get up to the line with you, but it also has a tendency to fall short, allowing a smash return, or to go long, ending up out of bounds.

   If your shot goes as planned, your partner should start moving up immediately to gain good court position at the non-volley zone *before your opponent hits the ball.* If the shot doesn't do what you wished, be prepared to move back (and your partner should stay where he is) to get the return.

Position 7

Your opponents are split, with one at the
non-volley zone and the other at the baseline.
You and your partner are both at the non-volley zone.
What shots might you make and why?

_____

_____

_____

_____

_____

Position 7: Answers

1. If the ball coming to you is high enough, smash it back near the feet of the close opponent.

2. If the ball isn't high enough to smash, hit a hard shot to the feet of the far opponent.

3. Dink the ball wide into the open area in front of the far opponent, hoping that he may not be able to get to the ball in time.

Position 8

Your opponents are both at the baseline.
You and your partner are both at the non-volley zone.
What shots might you make and why?

_____

_____

_____

_____

_____

Position 8: Answers

1. If the ball coming to you is high enough, smash it back to an open area on the court (trying for a shot that your opponents can't return) or toward the feet of either opponent. If the ball isn't high, hit a drive in the same directions. Remember that you have a lot of angles and room to play when you are at the net and your opponents are still in the backcourt.

2. Dink the ball (cross-court gives you more room). Hopefully your opponents will not be able to get up to the net fast enough to reach it. If you can start the dink with a drop volley, it is even more likely to be successful. If you let the ball bounce first, your opponents will have more time to get to the line and your dink will be less surprising. The drawback to the dink shot is that it brings your opponents to the non-volley zone, too.

Position 9

All players are at the non-volley zone.
What shots might you make and why?

Position 9: Answers

1. Dink the ball (cross-court is usually easiest since it gives the most room for the shot). Your opponents are already at the net anyway, so dinking can be a good strategy. Pat Kane says you should always dink if the ball is not high enough to smash, since doing anything else will probably put the ball into the net.

2. If the ball comes at you high enough, smash it back toward the feet of either opponent. If the ball isn't high, hit a hard drive toward the opponent directly across from you.

3. Lob the ball over either opponent's head. You can send it to center court, hoping some confusion may arise as to which one will go for the shot, or to the backhand of the player outside (more risky). Again, the goal is to send your opponents away from the non-volley zone, but the lob has a tendency to fall short, allowing a smash return, or to go long, ending up out of bounds.

Chapter 6

Playing Singles and Doubles

In most ways, pickleball is the same whether you're playing singles or doubles. There are some slight differences, however, that bear discussion.

Playing Singles

The largest difference between singles and doubles is the amount of energy required to play alone. Because you have to cover the entire court by yourself, you need more endurance to play a typical singles game. The rules are the same, and you still play to 11 points (winning by two in tournament play).

It's important to return to center court whenever possible after making a shot. Your opponent, of course, is trying to force you away from the center or out of bounds and keep you on the run. You are also trying to do the same to him.

What are the best strategies for singles play? Pat Kane, one of the top-ranked players in the U.S., says you should play to your opponent's backhand 80% of the time. Send forehand drives deep into your opponent's court and keep him back at the baseline. Aiming your shots cross-court gives you more room to keep the shot in bounds and will force your opponent to the outside to retrieve the ball.

Playing Doubles

Choosing a Partner

What are the qualities to look for in an "ideal" partner? The answer depends on you, your level of play, and the types of games you'll play together.

- **Your ideal partner should have approximately the same playing ability.** This allows both of you to play more or less equally during a game, rather than having one partner dominate play.

- **Choose a partner whose character and style of play complement yours.** If you are easily distracted, for example, don't choose someone who chatters incessantly. If you need encouragement to play your best, find someone who is happy and able to supply that. Make sure your playing rhythms are similar. If you move quickly, find a partner who does, too, or you'll find yourself wishing he would hurry along.

- **Make sure your goals for play are the same.** Obviously, it would be great if you could always win your games. Making winning your only goal is not realistic, however, and won't serve you in the long run. What goals might be good ones? To enjoy play. To learn something new each time you are together. To play better. You may not always achieve these goals, but having them will improve your play and will definitely improve your partnership since you'll be headed in the same direction together.

Court Position

Winning a point means that you will serve next from the other side of your court. You must switch sides of your court each time you make a point, but no rule says that your partner must switch sides or that you must remain where you are after serving. Some non-serving doubles partners actually stand to the right of their serving partner when the serve is being made from the even (or right) court—and then the server immediately moves to the odd (or left) court after service.

Why do this? Approximately 80 percent of the time, returned shots come down the middle of the court. If a left-handed player is in the odd court, the shot down the middle can pose a problem. Likewise, if a left-hander is in the even court and vice-versa, you may find that you need to have good communication to avoid both of you trying to go for the ball. Similarly, a right-handed player with a stronger forehand should be in the odd court, if possible, to cover the middle (and vice-versa for a left-hander).

If you examine your collective strengths as a doubles pair, you may find that you are better suited to playing on one court than another. Using the positioning strategy described above allows you to do that, despite where the server must stand, and is especially effective if one partner is significantly stronger in a particular way than the other. Here are some examples:

2   If both of you are right-handed, try positioning the partner with a stronger backhand in the even court and/or the partner with a stronger forehand in the odd court.

2   Position the left-handed partner in the odd court so that his topspin-enabled forehand can be used effectively as a service return.

2   Sometimes an injury can make it difficult for a player to cover one side as effectively as the other. The strategy above allows that player to always be positioned on his "good" side.

Communication Is the Key to Success

Most good doubles players communicate with each other frequently during a game. Some communicate after every point. Your communication might include encouragement, so your partner will remain confident (it also boosts your confidence when you encourage your partner), positive feedback, or specific suggestions about things you've noticed. Communication between partners is easier when you're doing well, but it is crucial when you are trying to come back after losing one or more points.

Communication by itself is not enough. You must communicate *well* for it to be of value. Start off the court by talking over your game plan: deciding who will chase lobs, which side you'll start from, who will serve first, who will handle overheads, who will cover the "down the middle" shots, etc.

Remember that you are *partners*—in the game together, for better or worse. Make it better by communicating positively with your partner. Much of what makes good communication has to do with creating the chemistry of a good partnership. It takes time, and there's no set way in which it can be done, since all of us are different. Some people respond well to a lot of information; others prefer an occasional comment. You and your partner must get to know each other. You need to know what to do when your partner feels bad or nervous. And before you can do anything about these feelings, you first have to learn to recognize them.

Your partner cannot read your mind. Do not assume anything. Don't leave anything to chance. If it is ever uncertain who should hit a ball, call "yours" or "mine." If it appears that your partner might play a ball that you think would be out, call "bounce it."

Lamenting poor shots or bad luck doesn't do anything positive and can be detrimental to a game that is going poorly.

Instead, make positive comments or discuss specific things you both might try to improve your game.

It's important that *both* of you communicate. Don't be timid or shy when it comes to making suggestions or calls that may improve your game. Give your partner suggestions when you think a certain kind of shot might be good, or when you notice something about your opponents that might be of value.

A good partner communicates well, both verbally and non-verbally, emotionally, and technically. Ensure that both of you are able to "read" each other well, and that your partner is not afraid to give or take constructive criticism when it is appropriate. You, as an ideal partner also, should always be happy to receive advice and act on it.

When the pressure is on, make sure you both talk *more*—not less. Don't be quiet or shy. Just as you will benefit from encouragement and suggestions about how your play might improve, so will your partner. Avoid destructive comments—even small ones—as these will weaken your play.

After you've been playing together for a while, discussing issues openly with your partner will become easier. Identify phrases or other things that annoy you on the court, and tell your partner. Knowing what to say or do (and what *not* to say or do) will be invaluable in helping you play better together.

While both partners will hopefully accept constructive criticism, remember to avoid making a critical remark when a positive one would achieve the same result. This is especially true during stressful moments, such as in the middle of a game. When things are not going well, you may not feel like making any type of comment, but that is exactly when you should. Don't be afraid to talk to your partner. Raise your collective spirits by commenting positively on what might go well, what you might try, or what might at least lighten things up during a difficult time.

Your partner is human. He will make mistakes. But don't make the mistake of undermining him by criticizing him, arguing with him about a play or call, or anything else that might come up, especially in front of your opponents. Instead, quietly suggest a way he might improve something that isn't working well, or suggest that he correct a call you know to be in error.

Don't underestimate the importance of good communication in doubles. If you communicate well, you're more likely to enjoy playing, and, if you enjoy the game, you're much more likely to play well.

Make Your Body Language Work for You

Body language is a large part of communication between people on the pickleball court as much as anywhere else. It is often overlooked because people don't consciously try to direct their body language. You can use body language like any other tool, and it can make a great difference in the way you play as well as the way your partner *and your opponents* react to you.

If you exude confidence, with your body relaxed yet ready and a smile on your face, your partner will feel better about you, and your opponents may not be as confident in their ability to overcome you. Instead, if your body language tells your partner that you are critical of him, or that you appear worried or disinterested, your game will suffer.

It's a proven fact that changing your body language can change your attitude. If your game isn't going as well as you'd like, consider changing your appearance so that you look like a winner. It can't hurt and certainly should help.

Trust Your Partner

If you are going for a ball and your partner says to "bounce it," you might consider letting it go, no matter whether you think the ball is going to be good. One of the people I spoke with said it's better to maintain trust and confidence between partners than to go for that ball, even if it ends up being in. He says you can almost always make up the point, but it's much harder to regain trust once it's lost.

Shadow Your Partner

Many partners will tell you that they benefit from a technique called "shadowing." When you are shadowing, you and your partner move as if you are connected by a cord that keeps you about ten feet apart. When your partner moves after a ball, you move, too, in the same general direction, staying about ten feet away. Likewise, when you move for a ball, your partner's movements follow yours at the same general distance.

Why? Because it reduces the number of times your opponents will find a hole between the two of you. When your partner is pulled to the sideline to return a ball, you will be covering the middle of the entire court, making it easier for you to go after most of your opponents' shots. It's true that this will leave some space on your side, but it's better to have your opponents aim over the higher part of the net and nearer the sidelines than it is to invite them to fire a relatively safe winner into the hole in the middle between you.

Figure 41. Shadowing your partner.

Shadowing your partner's movements will help your defense to remain consistent and strong. Shadowing works in all directions: forward, backward, right, and left. When you move up to the non-volley line, your partner should move also, keeping you both in a position of strength and avoiding making an opening between you. This is important: if one of you is up at the non-volley zone and the other is back at the baseline, you've created a large gap through which your opponent can send a ball that neither of you can return.

Similarly, if your partner moves to the backcourt to retrieve a ball, you should follow. Your partner has a reason for moving backward: either he's retrieving a deep shot or preparing to do so. He will be returning the shot from a defensive position, and both of you should be prepared for the opponent to slam a return back at you. Remain back until it's safe for both of you to move up again.

Poaching

Poaching is the method of moving in front of your partner to return a shot. Poaching is effective because it comes as a surprise to your opponents, allowing you to put away a shot that might otherwise be returned. Don't let it surprise your partner, however. Develop rules ahead of game time about how you'll handle poaching.

There are two kinds of poaching. One is opportunistic: a player at the non-volley zone spots a weak shot by an opponent and reaches or crosses in front of his partner to take advantage of it. The other occurs when both players execute a pre-planned switch of sides.

When you execute a pre-planned poach, follow through completely with the move. By doing this, your partner will be able to cover for you. If you and your partner *don't* switch sides, and your opponent returns the ball, one of your courts will be open and vulnerable.

With an opportunistic poach, the depth of your encroachment should determine whether or not you and your partner switch sides. If you only reach into your partner's territory by a foot or two, you can return to your own side faster than you could cross over. To avoid confusion, one player should yell "switch" if that is the intent.

If you're moving up from the backcourt, make sure you run toward the net to return your opponent's shot. Moving forward or diagonally allows you to return the ball sooner, which means you won't have to move as far to get to it. When poaching and moving up from the backcourt, don't run sideways—you want to be as close to the net as possible to hit your best shot. The goal of poaching is to end the rally.

Proper timing is essential when you are poaching. Try to start your poaching move when your opponent begins his forward swing. At that point, he is committed to his shot and probably won't be able to change direction.

General Tips

- **Practice together often to reinforce your techniques and to make them second nature in a game.** Make sure you treat your partner the same way in practice as in a game: with respect. Have faith in your partner. If you are the better player, you may occasionally poach a shot, since doing so can surprise your opponents. Don't monopolize the court, however. Allow your partner to take the shots that come to his side of the court, and trust that he will return them.

- **Unless your game is truly a friendly one, do not become "friends" with your opponents or feel sorry for them.** Also, make sure you stand up for your rights as a team. You might find that some players will try to take advantage of you or may not be as fair as they should be. Be fair with them, but don't allow them to take anything they haven't earned.

- **Watch your partner, at least when he is in front of you.** The players I talked with are divided on this point (of course!).

  Some say you should only watch your partner when he is in front of you and that you should keep your eyes on your opponents the rest of the time. They feel that your partner can take care of himself, and it's more important for you to be ready for your opponent's return shot than to know what your partner is doing.

  Others say that watching your partner will help you play better as a team. They believe that it's usually best to know where your partner is so you can shadow his movements and keep your defense strong. Bill Booth added, "it is impossible to fully anticipate and get in the best position for the play if you don't see the speed and trajectory of the shot that your partner is making. Imagine if you are at the line looking straight ahead and your partner is behind you and throws up a short lob. Ouch. All of a sudden, you might wish you'd anticipated that." He went on to say that the majority of people he's heard suggesting that you keep your eyes on your opponent are former tennis players and learned this from tennis instructors. He thought it might be because the risk of eye injury is significantly greater in tennis than in pickleball.

In part, it may depend upon how experienced you are and how good your peripheral vision is. When I play, I watch my partner, no matter where he is on the court. There are two reasons I do this. First, I feel it is more important for me to know what kind of shot my partner is making than to watch my opponents exclusively. I shift my focus when the time is right, and I do watch my opponents as soon as I know the speed and trajectory of the shot my partner just made. Knowing where the shot is going helps me prepare better for my opponent's reaction to that shot. Second, I am able to help with line calls for the balls coming to my partner. When you're going for a shot, you are far less able to judge with accuracy where the ball will land (or did land). Not only can I call him off a shot that I feel will end up out of bounds, but I can make the line calls for balls landing on our side of the court more accurately than he can when he's reaching for a return.

You'll have to judge what works best for you and your partner. However, the consensus is that it's wise at least to keep an eye out for your partner when he's in front of you and making a shot.

Chapter 7

Practice and Drills

Despite its sometimes nasty reputation, practice does make perfect (or nearly so) and, with pickleball at least, most people find that it's fun to do.

When you were learning to drive a car, you were awkward because you had to think about so many different things, all of which were new. After a while, driving became automatic, and now you don't think about *how* to drive the car—you just watch the traffic. The rest takes care of itself.

Practice is what made that happen. The same will occur in pickleball (or anything else) if you do it enough. If your preparation and strokes become automatic, you will be able to concentrate on where you want the ball to go and you will win more rallies.

Remember, though: *the things you practice will become ingrained.* This means that you should *not* practice the wrong things because it will be much harder to unlearn them later.

Whatever your goal, practice, if done correctly, will get you there. First, determine what you need or want to do. Second, make sure you're doing it correctly. Most practice requires another person to help you by throwing or hitting balls to you.

The easiest way to practice is with others in a casual setting. Spend time hitting balls to each other, noting anything that might improve your play. Work on returning different types of shots (lob,

---

drop volley, etc.) and on directing the ball accurately where you want it to go.

If you need to practice alone, you can do so by hitting serves, practicing spins, overhead smashes (as if hitting a serve in tennis), and more by hitting many balls over a net. Alternatively, if you have a wall available (or better still, a handball court or something similar), you can tape a line at net height and practice hitting to spots on the walls.

Before you begin practicing, be sure to warm up completely. Do it this time. Do it every time.

The players I spoke with said their practice fell into three main categories:

1. Correcting something that isn't going well;
2. Perfecting a skill;
3. Doing drills to stay on top of things.

1. Correcting Part of Your Game

Some players commented that elements of their game "disappeared" from time to time. Suddenly they weren't hitting overheads properly or their serves weren't accurate anymore. Have someone watch you and suggest what you might try to change, or pay attention to your stroke, timing, and/or your body position to figure out what the problem might be.

Once you've identified the problem, practice doing it the right way (or at least a different way), concentrating on only that thing. In a little while, the "new" method should become a habit and you won't have to think about it anymore.

2. Perfecting a Skill

Many people use drills to help them become better in a certain area. Players mentioned these areas most: 1) dinking, 2) serves or groundstrokes, and 3) backhand weakness. Here are some fun ways to practice the first two.

Back Ball

This is a game where players stay near the baseline and must let the ball bounce before hitting it. This game improves the accuracy of ground strokes and people say it's fun.

Dink-A-Dink or Short Court

As the names suggest, in this game, the non-volley zone line is considered the baseline and balls hit beyond that line are "out." Playing this dinking game is great for practicing the dink in a competitive situation. Players who don't yet feel comfortable with the soft game can use this method to get better at it quickly.

3. Backhand Practice

As for practicing backhands, the best answer is to have someone hit balls to your backhand side repeatedly until it gets easier. Again, you have to analyze what you're doing in order to decide what other things to try. Perhaps the standard backhand you imported from tennis just isn't working anymore. Is your wrist too stiff? Are you bending your body into your swing or remaining upright? Get someone who can really analyze all the elements of your stroke to watch and critique your play. Then try something different.

What Else Should You Do?

The exercises presented here are examples—suggestions to get you started. Adapt them to the things you need or want to work on.

Imagine or actually lay out targets on the court across the net as shown in the diagram that follows. Targets can be many types of objects, such as cones, plastic discs, etc.

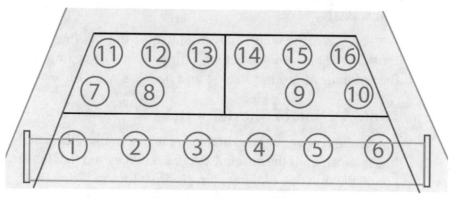

Figure 42. Practice targets.

Practice hitting to these target positions using the shots described below. You don't need to do all of them—these are examples of some of the different shots you can practice. Feel free to order them as you wish, leaving out some, adding others, or changing the repetitions. The instructions assume you have a friend helping you practice. If not, you can throw the ball for yourself, letting it bounce where necessary.

Hitting from the Baseline

- **Forehand crosscourt from corner position.**
  Hit one forehand to positions 11 through 16, first from the even court and then the odd court.

- **Serving directional practice.**
  Serve one ball to positions 11 through 16, first from the even court and then the odd court.

- **Backhand crosscourt from corner position.**
  Hit one backhand to positions 16 through 11, first from the even court and then the odd court.

- **Forehand short angles.**
  Hit one forehand to positions 7 through 10, first from the even court and then the odd court.

- **Backhand short angles.**
  Hit one backhand to positions 7 through 10, first from the even court and then the odd court.

- **Forehand crosscourt.**
  Standing in the middle of the baseline, hit a forehand shot to positions 11 through 16.

- **Backhand crosscourt.**
  From the middle of the baseline, hit two backhand shots each to positions 16 through 11.

- **Forehand lob.**
  Standing in the middle of the baseline, hit a forehand lob to positions 11 through 16.

- **Backhand lob.**
  From the middle of the baseline, hit a backhand lob to positions 16 through 11.

- **Overhead smash accuracy.**
  Have your helper throw or hit the ball to you in different areas of the court. Run forward and hit two overheads each to positions 16 through 11.

- **Forehand drop accuracy.**
  Hit a forehand drop shot to positions 1 through 6, from the midcourt, first on the right and then on the left.

- **Backhand drop accuracy.**
  Hit a backhand drop shot to positions 6 through 1, from the midcourt, first on the right and then on the left.

Hitting from the Non-Volley Zone Line

- **Forehand overhead smash accuracy.**
  Standing on the midline of the court, hit two forehand overhead smashes each to positions 7 through 10.

- **Backhand overhead smash accuracy.**
  From the midline of the court, hit two backhand overhead smashes each to positions 10 through 7.

- **Overhead smash "on the move."**
  Have your partner hit the ball slightly over your head. Standing on the midline of the court, sidestep backwards to get under the ball, and hit two overheads each to positions 11 through 16.

Practicing with a Wall

I sometimes practice with a wall, and I can tell you that it provides a demanding workout. Sue Gardiner said that she and a friend devised certain drills that they felt were quite valuable to their game. Practicing with walls is not just for when you can't get to a court. It really can be a good way to practice since the ball (almost) always comes back your way, making it easier to keep going.

Tape or chalk a line on the wall(s) at net height so you'll know where to hit the ball. If you can work with a partner, you'll enjoy this practice even more, and you can take turns getting the rebounds from the wall.

Here are some suggested shots to practice and how you might use one or more walls to work on them.

- **Volley.**
  Stand 4 to 6 feet from the wall and practice volleying both forehand and backhand. Then move back to about 8 feet and try it again.

- **Overhead smash.**
  Toss the ball in the air and smash it to the wall (from about 10 feet away). This is very similar to serving in tennis. The reason to do this at a wall is that the ball comes back to you so you can practice again.

- **Forehand and backhand with corner walls (see Figure 43).**
  Hit a forehand to the right corner wall so that it bounces onto the left wall before coming back to you. When it returns, hit it with a backhand so that it hits the left wall first and then bounces on the right. You can keep this up until you miss (or the wall does!).

Figure 43. Corner wall practice example.

Chapter 8

The Mental Game

When you were very young, you learned by watching and emulating what you saw. You tried different things and saw what worked. You didn't chide yourself for things you didn't know or things you'd learned incorrectly. You managed to pick up a lot of knowledge very quickly.

When you first start playing pickleball, you also learn very quickly. After you've been at it for a while, though, you may find that your skills actually seem to get worse and that your play is not as good as it once was. This may be caused by high expectations of yourself that pressure you to equal or better a previous performance. When you were first learning, everything you did was good: it was better than when you didn't play well or at all. If you can return to the naïve state you had as a novice player, despite what you know now, whatever your level, you will do better.

W. Timothy Gallwey has written a fine book called *Inner Tennis* in which he discusses what he calls the Inner Game. The examples he gives are not specific to pickleball, but the information can be applied to nearly any sport, or even to life in general. His book begins, "A tennis player first confronts the Inner Game when he discovers that there is an opponent inside his own head more formidable than the one across the net." If you are interested in learning about how to tame your mind and play better, please read this book.

We all know that worrying is a fire that fuels itself. Once you start to worry, or if you feel nervous about making a mistake, chances are you *will* make that mistake, causing you to worry more. "I'm probably going to miss this shot..." "Will we be able to win even one game?" "I've got to stop hitting into the net..." "I can't believe we're down 8 to 3..." "My practice game is always better than the real one..." How many times during a game do you find yourself thinking this way?

Then there's fear. Fear of losing, fear of not doing as well as you might, fear of looking bad—the list goes on and on. How about frustration, self-consciousness, poor concentration, and more.

When I was interviewing players for this book, Vic Avery told me, "I'm just like everyone else. I get mad after missing an easy shot. So I allow myself a few seconds to make a comment to myself. I say, 'Next point,' and my concentration shifts to getting ready for that. If I'm receiving, I think, 'Where will I return the serve if I have options?' If I'm serving, I clear my mind so I'll be ready for the best option after the return."

Some players said they create affirmations or mantras that help them to diffuse the worry or nervousness during a game. Practice these affirmations along with your shots and you may find that they will work well during a game because they're second nature. Practice. Then, once the game starts, you will know that you have done everything you can to prepare and, as a result, you will be more relaxed and will perform better.

Here are some ideas that may help you stay ahead of yourself and control the mental side of pickleball.

- Keep a happy, positive attitude. It's much easier to change your attitude or outlook than to change your game. Just as your game can affect your attitude, your attitude does affect your play. You will do better if you are positive, happy, and believe you will play well.

- Concentrate. Keep focused on the actions occurring at this moment—not the last point, or something someone said, or things you believe you're not doing correctly. Instead, concentrate on watching the ball or some other aspect of play. Keep focused on your game plan.

- Relax. You'll be surprised how much this one thing can do to improve your entire game.

- Ignore the score. Apart from saying the score before serving, it's better to ignore it. Worrying about being down 10 to 4 isn't going to help anything. Remember that last time you were down 10 to 4 you came back to win. Be positive and think only about the next rally.

- If things aren't going well, or you're making mistakes, don't try to make the best shot. Instead concentrate only on making sure you get the shot back over the net. Keep the rally going. Let your opponents make the faults.

- Practice self confidence. In many of the books that discuss how to succeed in other fields, the authors stress the importance of self esteem or self confidence. It may seem silly, but it works: tell yourself (aloud) that you play well (in present tense), that you can win, that you enjoy pickleball. This type of affirmation "sticks" after a while, and the more you believe it, the more likely you are to find that it's true.

- Use positive thinking. Picture yourself on the court with a medal around your neck or holding your paddle high in the air when they call your name as the game or tournament winner. Do this over and over, and you'll convince yourself it can happen.

- Don't try too hard. You've practiced, and you know you can do well when the pressure is off. Your body knows better than you do what is required to make the perfect shot. Let your natural instincts (honed with practice) take over and you'll find and make the shots that make pickleball an easy sport.

Chapter 9

Safety, Etiquette, and Ethics

Etiquette on the pickleball court may not be essential, but I much prefer playing with people who have good court manners. The written and unwritten rules of court conduct lead to better and happier play.

I consider ethics to be very important on the court, however. By ethics, I mean such things as calling a shot the way you believe it was (not as you wish it might have been), announcing faults your partner didn't see, correcting him if he makes a "bad" call, and not cheating. There will always be disagreements about calls made during a game. Such things are not usually critical in casual play. Playing honorably, however, is a mark of character I would encourage, no matter what the stakes.

While etiquette and ethics are preferred on the court, I hold that safety is a must. The tips given here for safety are more important than the rest, so they're listed first. Being safe means avoiding injuries and having fun.

Safety on the Court

- If a ball comes into your court from another game, hold your paddle or other hand[8] up in the air and say "ball" loudly enough that the other players can hear you and play will stop. Likewise, if your ball goes into another court where people are playing, call "ball" loudly enough for them to hear. Stepping on an unseen pickleball can cause a player to fall, and such accidents can result in serious injuries. It doesn't matter whether you believe everyone has seen the ball, or if you feel silly calling it—call it anyway. Always err on the side of safety.

- If the courts are slippery, do not play. Check an outdoor court surface by pressing down on it with the toe of your shoe. If moisture comes to the surface, wait to play until the courts have dried further. Indoor courts can be wiped down, if necessary, before play.

- Any stray dirt, gravel, or leaves should be removed from outdoor courts before play begins.

- Items such as extra paddles, gym bags, or clothing, either on the court or outside court boundaries where players may step to retrieve a ball in play, can be a hazard if stepped on and should be removed.

- Don't leave extra pickleballs lying around on the court surface. Even if you think they are out of the way (in a corner or under a bench), a gust of wind can carry them onto the court, causing a hazard.

- If you are playing on a homemade court or other area that is not specifically designated for sports, be sure that all

8. There are three acceptable means of signaling "not ready" per the rules: raise your paddle in the air above your head, raise your non-paddle hand, or turn around. In the case of signaling a ball entering into your court, use either of the first two signals.

obstacles, sharp objects, or other hazards are removed as much as possible from the playing area. Pad any sharp or hard items in the playing area that cannot be removed. Be sure all players know about possible hazards before starting play.

- If you wear prescription lenses, get a pair of unbreakable prescription sports lenses for use when playing pickleball. Protective eyewear might be a good idea if you don't wear glasses. Wilson makes an inexpensive set of goggles (available at sporting goods stores and some discount chain stores). These will not enhance your appearance, but they might save your eyesight or make you feel more confident if you are worried about being hit by a ball.

Etiquette on the Court

- If you must cross through one court area to get to another, do not walk behind people while they are playing unless absolutely necessary. Wait until the rally has ended, and then walk briskly through the court.

- If a rally has not yet begun and you are not ready to play, hold your paddle up in the air or turn around so your back is to the other players. You are allowed to interrupt the game for a short time without penalty (for example, to tie your shoe or to remove something from the court). If you must interrupt the game for a longer period, call a time out.

- Before serving, make sure the opponent who will receive the ball is ready and facing you. Then call the score. Leave a few seconds for any questions or corrections to the score before starting the serve.

- If the server calls the score incorrectly and does not leave enough time to correct it then, some people say you should wait until the rally is over and then correct the score. Doing so earlier would disrupt either the serve or the return, or both. Pat Kane disagrees, however, saying that you'll be concentrating on the fact that the score was wrong during the whole point, although this is probably not an issue except in competitive play. Pat says you should stop play and have the correct score called and then continue.

- Pay attention to the game and particularly to the score. This helps to avoid disagreements or delays while you figure out what the score should be and makes the game more fun for everyone.

- In casual play outside when the sun is out or it's windy, try to remember to switch sides when one side has half the number of points toward game. For example, if you're playing to 11 points, change sides when one team has 6 points. If you don't remember at that time, do it as soon as you do remember, since it helps to make the game more fair.

- When the rally is over and you have the ball your opponent needs to serve, return it *to* him, not just *toward* him.

- Keep your temper. I've seen players become angry, whether at themselves or other players, and throw their paddles around the court. Remember: you're out there to have fun.

Ethics and Sportsmanship

Good sportsmanship makes the game more fun for everyone. We all want to win, but not at the expense of sacrificing our ethics or our principles.

- Except in tournament play, there are no line judges or referees to call faults. Each side, therefore, is required to call the faults that occur on their side of the net. This means that you must determine whether balls that have been hit by your opponents are in or out. Call the balls fairly. Remember, your opponents will be doing the same for you.

- Do not call faults that occur on the other side of the net unless those players ask what you saw.

- The player who is returning the ball has a much harder time determining whether or not that ball is good. In doubles play, watch the ball and help your partner by making the call.

- If your partner calls a ball out, but you know it was in, you should correct this call. If possible, tell your partner that you disagree with his call, and let *him* correct his error. If this isn't possible, declare that the ball is good. Either way, the call will go to your opponents, but the first method helps preserve team unity in everyone's eyes.

- If you volley the ball and step into or on the line of the non-volley zone, call the fault. If you see your partner fault in the non-volley zone, call the fault.

- When signaling your partner that a ball is not going to land in the court, try saying "let it go" or "bounce it" instead of calling "out" or "wide." This way, you're suggesting a course of action rather than declaring a line call on a ball that hasn't yet bounced.

- If you believe a ball will bounce out but has a chance of being in, return the ball, if possible. If it does bounce out, call it immediately before the hit or as soon as possible after the hit. Note that this is true only for balls that *bounce*. If you volley a ball that otherwise would have bounced out, the ball is still in play. The best course of action with any ball that you believe will be out is to let it bounce before hitting it.

Chapter 10

Notes about Tournament Play

Complete rules about tournaments can be found in the pickleball rules on the USAPA web site (http://www.usapa.org). I thought it might be helpful, however, to include some notes about certain rules that may help you play better in your next tournament.

Referees

The referee is the authority who certifies that the match is played properly. The tasks of a referee will vary, depending on whether or not line judges are available and how the tournament is structured.

Typically, the referee keeps track of and calls the score before each rally and ensures that the rules of the game are followed.

If no line judges are available, it is usually the referee's responsibility to make line calls only for the non-volley zone. In this case, players are responsible for making the rest of the line calls on their side of the court, whether it be foot faults during a serve or calling a ball in or out.

If you are unsure about whether or not a ball was good, you may ask the referee what he saw. If you do this, it's important to know that the referee's ruling is binding. If you don't like his call, you're stuck with it. Often, the referee will tell you he didn't see the play well enough to call it, since he is usually busy watching for non-volley zone line and other rules violations.

Tournament Rules

Tournament play is different from friendly games in a number of ways. Here are some specifics to keep in mind when you are playing in a tournament.

- **Questioning the Referee.** You may *not* question a referee's call, but you may request a clarification of the rule used for the judgment. For example, you might not realize you had stepped into the non-volley zone during a volley. While you cannot dispute or question the call the referee made, you may ask what rule was violated and expect an explanation.

- **Replays.** Many replays occur in friendly games. In tournaments, however, only a few situations result in a replay:

- A referee who called a non-volley zone or other rules violation in error.

- Interference from a ball, player, or other object on the court.

- A server serves the ball while an opponent is signaling not ready.

- A cracked or broken ball that, in the judgment of the referee, affected the play.

- **Line calls.** You should only call the lines on your own side of the court. This is proper etiquette in friendly play also but is especially important during a tournament. Make your calls immediately, before the ball is hit by your opponent, no matter how obvious they may seem. Making no call means that the ball is good and is still in play. Any ball that cannot be called "out" is presumed to be good.

If you believe your opponents made an incorrect line call, you can appeal to the referee (simply say "appeal"). If the referee saw the ball clearly in, he can overrule the call. If not, it stands. Appeals are common in tournament play, and should cause no hard feelings on either side.

- **Technical warnings and fouls.** The referee may call technical fouls. These can occur for various reasons described below. When a technical foul is called, one point is added to the score of the offending player's opponent(s). If play is not immediately resumed, the referee may end the match, forfeiting in favor of the offending player's opponent(s). If a player or team receives two technical fouls during a match or tournament, that match will be forfeit and that player or team will be excluded from tournament play.

Actions that may result in technical fouls are:

- Profanity.
- Excessive argument.
- Threats to any player or referee.
- Purposely breaking the ball or striking the ball between rallies.
- Delaying the game, either by taking too much time during time-outs and between games, excessive questioning of the referee, or excessive or unnecessary appeals.
- Throwing the paddle (note that if a paddle strikes another player, referee, or spectator, or if it damages the court or facility, the foul is automatic).
- Any other behavior that is deemed dangerous to another player, spectator, or referee.

If a player's behavior is not severe enough to warrant a technical foul, the referee will typically issue a technical warning instead.

Choosing Side or Serve

If you win the choice of side or serve, which should you choose? It depends on several factors, as well as personal preference. Here are some guidelines.

- Choose serve if the sun or wind are not problems and if you are confident with your play.

- Also choose serve if your opponent has not had much time to warm up.

- Choosing serve puts you in the greatest control of the match when the game begins.

- Choose side if you feel that the sun or wind will affect your play.

- If you have the choice of side and the sun is a factor, play on the sunny side first. If you take the sunny side and do well, you'll boost your mental game knowing that the next game (or half) will be played more easily. If you take the sunny side first and don't do as well, you can attribute your lesser score to the effects of the sun and boost your mental game, knowing that you'll have it easier in the next round of play.

- If you have the choice of side, and the wind is a factor, play with the wind. This requires that you soften your shots so they stay in bounds. You can usually play softer, but you can't always add more power. Playing against the wind can be difficult because you must hit harder, which sometimes means sacrificing accuracy. More than some of the previous choices, this decision depends on the type of player you are and whether or not you tend to hit the ball long or short. You may also wish to assess if the wind is increasing or decreasing, and choose your side accordingly.

References

Baker, Scott, *et al*. The Lesson Lounge. Last accessed 30 August 2005. http://www.tennis4you.com/lesson-lounge/lessonlounge.htm

Blaskower, Pat. *The Art of Doubles: Winning Tennis Strategies.* Cincinnati, OH: Better Way Books, 1994.

Braden, Vic. *Maximizing Your Tennis Potential.* ESPN Home Video, 1989.

Braden, Vic. "Vic's Tips: The Vic Braden Tennis College." Last accessed 30 August 2005. http://www.vicbraden.com/vics.html

Curtis, Joyce M. *Pickle-Ball for Player and Teacher.* Second Edition. Englewood, CO: Morton Publishing Company, 1989.

Douglas, Paul. *101 Essential Tips: Tennis.* New York: DK Publishing, Inc., 1995.

Friedenberg, Mark. *The Official Pickleball Handbook.* Tacoma, WA: PB Master, 1999.

Gallwey, W. Timothy. *Inner Tennis: Playing the Game.* New York: Random House, Inc., 1976.

Nicholas Institute of Sports Medicine and Athletic Trauma. "Physical Therapy Corner: Tennis Elbow - Lateral and Medial Epicondylitis." http://www.nismat.org/ptcor/tennis elbow/

SportsKnowHow.com. "Pickleball History." http://www.sportsknowhow.com/pickleball/history/pickleball-history.shtml

USA Pickleball Association (USAPA) Official Tournament Rulebook

The following rules are reproduced with permission from the United States of America Pickleball Association (USAPA). The USAPA published its first rule book in March, 1984, and several revisions have been made since then. Revisions to the rules are now made yearly. Many of these changes are in response to player inquiries or new situations that arise during play. I have included some new rules and rule changes that were not yet in effect at the time this book was printed but which will take effect in May, 2008 (listed as such in the text). Please check the USAPA web site (usapa.org) to ensure you have the most recent version.

- Feb. 3, 2007: Revised sections 2 and 4.
- May 1, 2007: Revised sections 5 and 6. Section 18 revised and moved to section 6.D.
- November 1, 2007: Revised sections 7-15. Sections 16 (Playing Tips) and 17 (Game Variations) were deleted. Added new rule 6.D.12 and revised rule 4.F.5. Added new paragraph on the cover page regarding non-sanctioned tournament play. Revised paragraph 2.A.2 regarding total playing area of 34 x 64. Revised definition of "Hinder." Added new definitions for "Let," "Permanent Object," and "Service Court."
- January 14, 2008: List of Approved Events in section 15.B moved to the rankings document.
- May 1, 2008: Added paragraphs 4.I.4 and 12.L and revised section 13.

Please note also that certain clubs and some tournaments use rules that are different from the ones printed here in various ways. Make sure you know the local rule variants, if any, before playing in a tournament in a new location.

Contents

Section 1: The Game

Pickleball is a simple paddle game, playing a special perforated, slow-moving ball over a tennis type net, on a badminton-sized court.

The ball is served underhand, without bouncing it off the court, and is served diagonally to the opponent's service zone.

Points are scored by the serving side only and occur when the opponent faults (fails to return ball, hits ball out of bounds, etc.). The server continues to serve, alternating service courts, until server faults.

The first side scoring 11 points and leading by at least a 2-point margin wins. For example, if both sides are tied at 10 points, then play continues until one side wins by 2 points.

Unique Pickleball Features

- **Double Bounce Rule.** Following serve, each side must make at least one groundstroke prior to volleying ball (hitting it before it has bounced).

- **Non-Volley Zone.** A player cannot volley a ball while standing within the non-volley zone.

Section 2: Court and Equipment

Revised 2006

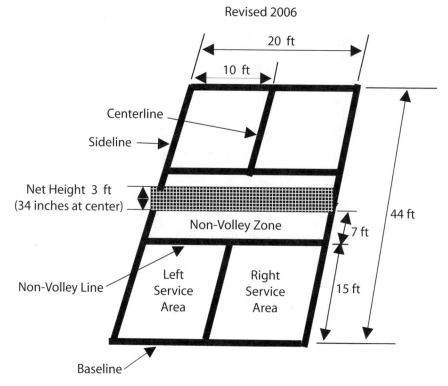

Figure 2-1   The Court

2.A   Court Specifications. The dimensions and measurements for the standard pickleball court are:

    2.A.1   The court shall be a rectangle 20 feet wide (6.10 m) and 44 feet long (13.41 m) for both singles and doubles matches. See Figure 2-1.

    2.A.2   A total playing area 30 feet wide (9.14 m) and 60 feet long (18.28 m) is the minimum size that is recommended. A total size of 34 feet (10.36 m) by 64 feet (19.5 m) is preferred.

    2.A.3   Court measurements shall be made to the outside of the lines. The lines should be 2 inches (5.1 cm) wide and the same color, clearly contrasting with the color of the court surface.

2.B **Lines and Areas.** The lines and areas of the standard pickleball court are:

    2.B.1 **Baselines.** The baselines are the lines parallel to the net at each end of the court.

    2.B.2. **Sidelines.** The sidelines are the lines perpendicular to the net on each side of the court.

    2.B.3. **Non-Volley Line.** The non-volley line is the line on each side of the net between the sidelines and parallel to the net. These lines are located 7 feet (2.13 m) from the net.

    2.B.4. **Non-Volley Zone.** The non-volley zone is the area on each side of the net between the non-volley line and the net.

    2.B.5. **Centerline.** The centerline is the line on each side of the net bisecting the area between the non-volley line and the baseline.

    2.B.6. **Service Courts.** The service courts are the areas on either side of the centerline, bounded by the non-volley line and the baseline.

2.C **Net Specifications.**

    2.C.1. **Material.** The net may be made of any open, meshed fabric material.

    2.C.2. **Net Size.** The net length shall be at least 20 feet (6.1 m) extending from one sideline to the other. The net width shall be at least 2½ feet (0.8 m).

    2.C.3. **Mesh Size.** The net's mesh size must be sufficiently small to prevent a ball from passing through it.

    2.C.4. **Height.** The net shall be suspended over the center of the court and shall be 36 inches (0.914 m) high at the sidelines and 34 inches (0.86 m) high at the center of the court.

    2.C.5. **Center Strap.** A center strap may be placed at the center of the net to enable easy adjustment to the 34 in. (0.86 m) requirement at center.

2.C.6. **Net Edge.** The top of the net should be edged with a 2-inch (5.1 cm) white binding over a cord or cable running through the binding. This binding must rest upon the cord or cable.

2.C.7. **Posts.** Net posts should be placed outside the sidelines. Recommended height of the post is 36 inches (0.914 m) and recommended placement is 12 inches (30.48 cm) from the sideline.

2.D Ball Specifications.

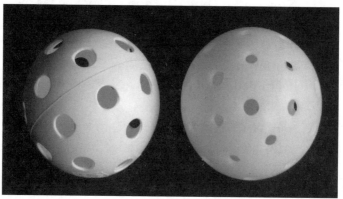

Figure 2-2.

The ball pictured on the left of Figure 2-2 is customarily used for indoor play and the ball pictured on the right is customarily used for outdoor play. However, either ball is acceptable for indoor or outdoor play.

2.D.1. **Construction.** The standard ball shall be made of durable plastic material molded with a smooth surface and free of texturing.

2.D.2. **Size.** The official ball shall be 27/8 inches (7.3 cm) to 3 inches (7.62 cm) in diameter.

2.D.3. **Weight.** The ball shall weigh between 0.8 and 1.02 oz (21 and 29 grams).

2.D.4. **Design.** Spacing of holes and overall design of the ball must conform to the straight flight characteristics required for play. Balls that fly or bounce erratically shall not be used.

2.D.5. **Approval.** The Tournament Director will choose the tournament ball. Balls approved for play in any USAPA-sanctioned tournament must be named on the official USAPA list of approved balls.

2.E Paddle Specifications.

2.E.1 **Material.** The paddle may be made of any material judged safe.

2.E.2. **Surface.** The paddle playing surface shall not contain holes, indentations, rough texturing, tape, or any objects or features that allow a player to impart additional or increased spin on the ball.

2.E.2.a. **Paint.** The surface may be painted but must otherwise adhere to the general surface requirements.

2.E.2.b. **Depictions.** Any writing or pictures on the paddle must be in good taste.

2.E.3. **Size.** The combined length and width including any edge guard and butt cap shall not exceed 23¾ inches (60.3 cm). The most common paddle measurement is approximately 8 inches (20.32 cm) wide by 15¾ inches (40 cm) long. There is no restriction on paddle thickness.

2.E.4. **Weight.** There is no restriction on paddle weight.

2.E.5. **Alterations.** Homemade or modified paddles are acceptable so long as they meet the size and surface specifications.

2.E.6. **Violation.** If a paddle violates the above rules, the Tournament Director has the authority to enforce a paddle change. If the player in violation refuses to change the paddle, the Director may declare a forfeiture of the match.

2.F. **Clothing.**

2.F.1. **Color.** Clothing may be of any color.

2.F.2. **Safety/Distraction.** A player may be required to change wet, extremely loose- fitting, or otherwise distracting garments.

2.F.3. **Depictions.** Insignias, pictures, and writing on the clothing must be in good taste.

2.F.4. **Shoes.** Shoes must have soles that do not mark or damage the court's playing surface.

2.F.5. **Violation.** If a player's clothing violates these rules, the Tournament Director has the authority to enforce clothing changes. If the player refuses, the Director may declare a forfeiture of the match.

Section 3: Definitions

3.A. **Carry** - Hitting the ball in such a way that it does not bounce away from the paddle but tends to be carried along on the face of the paddle during its forward motion.

3.B. **Cross-court** - The court diagonally opposite your court.

3.C. **Dead Ball** - A dead ball is declared after a fault. See fault.

3.D. **Dink Shot** - A soft shot that is intended to arc over the net and land within the non-volley zone.

3.E. **Double Bounce** - A ball that bounces more than once, on one side, before it is returned.

3.F. **Double Hit** - One side hitting the ball twice before it is returned over net. Double hits may occur by one player or could involve both players on a team.

3.G. **Drop Shot** - A groundstroke shot that falls short of the opponent's position.

3.H. **Drop Shot Volley** - A volley shot that is designed to "kill" the speed of the ball and return it short, near the net, to an opponent positioned at or near the baseline. This shot is especially effective when initiated close to the non-volley line.

3.I. **Fault** - A fault is any action that stops play or creates a rules violation.

3.J. **Groundstroke** - Hitting the ball after one bounce.

3.K. **Half Volley** - A groundstroke shot where the paddle contacts the ball immediately after it bounces from the court and before the ball rises to its potential height.

3.L. **Hinder** - Any element or occurrence that affects play. Examples: a stray ball that enters the court or people who disrupt play by walking across the court.

3.M. **Let** - A serve that hits the net cord and lands in the service court. Let may also refer to a rally that must be replayed for any reason.

3.N. **Lob** - A shot that returns the ball as high and deep as possible, forcing the opposing side back to the baseline.

3.O. **Non-Volley Zone** - The section of court adjacent to the net in which you cannot volley the ball. It includes all lines surrounding the zone.

3.P. **One Hand Out** - A term used to describe the condition when a serving team loses the first of its two allocated serves.

3.Q. **Overhead Slam/Smash** - A hard, overhand shot usually resulting from an opponent's lob, high return, or high bounce.

3.R. **Passing Shot** - A volley or groundstroke shot that is aimed at a distance from the player and is designed to prevent return of the ball (e.g., a line drive close to sideline).

3.S. **Permanent Object** - Any object near the court or hanging over the court that interferes with the flight of the ball.

3.T. **Rally** - Continuous play that occurs after the serve and before a fault.

3.U. **Replays** - Any rallies that are replayed for any reason without the awarding of a point or a side out.

3.V. **Service Court** - The areas on either side of the centerline, bounded by the non-volley line and the baseline.

3.W. **Side Out** - Declared after one side loses its service and other side is awarded service.

3.X. **Technical Foul** - The referee is empowered to add one point to a player's score or a team's score when, in the referee's judgment, the opponent is being overly and deliberately abusive.

3.Y. **Volley** - Hitting the ball in the air, during a rally, before the ball has a chance to bounce onto the court.

Section 4: Service Rules (Revised 5/1/08)

4.A. **Serve Motion.** The serve must be made with an underhand stroke so that contact with the ball is made below waist level.

> 4.A.1. Underhand Defined. The arm must be moving in an upward arc and the paddle head shall be below the wrist when it strikes the ball.

4.B. **Server Position.** The server must keep both feet behind the baseline during the serve with at least one foot on the court surface or ground at the time the ball is struck. The serve must be made while the server's feet are within the confines of the serving area. These confines lie behind the serving court baseline and on or between the imaginary lines extended from the court centerline and each sideline.

4.C. **The Serve.** The ball must be struck before it hits the court surface. The ball must land in the opponent's crosscourt (diagonally opposite court) service court.

> 4.C.1. **Placement.** The serve must clear the net and the non-volley line and land in the opponent's service court. The serve may land on any service court line except the non-volley line.

> 4.C.2. **Interference.** If the serve clears the net and the receiver or the receiver's partner interferes with the flight of the ball on the serve, it is a point for the serving team.

4.D. **Service Foot Fault.** During the serve, when the ball is struck, the server's feet shall not:

> 4.D.1. Touch the area outside the imaginary extension of the sideline.

> 4.D.2. Touch the area outside the imaginary extension of the centerline.

> 4.D.3. Touch the court, including the baseline.

4.E. **Service Faults.** During the service, it is a fault if:

> 4.E.1. The server misses the ball when trying to hit it. If the ball lands on the ground without the server swinging at the ball, it is not a fault.

4.E.2. The served ball touches any permanent object before it hits the ground. Permanent objects include the ceiling, walls, fencing, lighting fixtures, net posts, the stands and seats for spectators, the referee, line judges, spectators (when in their recognized positions) and all other objects around and above the court.

4.E.3. The served ball touches the server or server's partner, or anything the server or server's partner is wearing or holding.

4.E.4. The served ball lands on the non-volley line.

4.E.5. The served ball hits the net and lands on the non-volley line or inside the non-volley zone.

4.E.6. The served ball lands outside the service court.

4.E.7. The served ball hits the net and lands outside the service court.

4.F. **Service Lets.** The serve is a let and will be replayed if:

4.F.1. The serve touches the net, strap, or band, and is otherwise good and lands in the service court.

4.F.2. The ball is served when the receiver is not ready.

4.F.3. The served ball hits the net and strikes the receiver or the receiver's partner.

4.F.4. The referee or any player calls a time out because an object (a ball, another court's player, a spectator, etc.) causes a distraction by coming within the playing area.

4.F.5. The referee or a player may call a let. If the serve is appealed to the referee and the referee clearly saw that the serve did not touch the net, then a point is awarded to the serving team.

USAPA Comment: There is no limit to the number of lets a server may serve.

4.G. **The Receiver.** The receiver is the player diagonally opposite from the server. In doubles, this position corresponds to the player's score and starting position. There is no restriction on the receiver's position.

4.H. **Double Bounce Rule.** The serve and the service return must be allowed to bounce before striking the ball. That is, each side must play a groundstroke on the first shot following the serve. After the initial groundstrokes have been made, play may include volleys.

4.I. **Readiness.** Serves shall not be made until the receiver is ready and the score has been called. The score shall be called after both the server and the receiver have returned to their respective positions.

   4.I.1. **Not Ready Signals.** The receiver must use one of the following to signal that he or she is not ready to receive the serve: 1) raising the paddle above his or her head, 2) raising the non-paddle hand above his or her head, or 3) completely turning his or her back to the server.

   4.I.2. **Doubles.** When calling the score in doubles, the referee does not have to wait for the receiver's partner or the server's partner to be ready. It is the receiver's responsibility to signal not ready for his or her partner.

   4.I.3. **In Motion.** Once the server starts the serving motion, the receiver cannot become not ready or call a time-out.

   4.I.4. **Wrong Score Called.** If the referee calls the wrong score, any player may stop play at any time before the return of serve to ask for a correction. A player that interrupts play after the return of serve will have committed a fault and shall lose the rally. A player that interrupts play after the serve when there was not an error in the score will have committed a fault and shall lose the rally.

4.J. **The 10-Second Rule.** The "10-second rule" applies to both server and receiver, each of whom is allowed up to 10 seconds after the score is called to serve or be ready to receive. It is the server's responsibility to look and be certain that the receiver is ready to receive serve.

   4.J.1. After one technical warning has been issued by the referee, further delays on the part of the server or the receiver exceeding 10 seconds shall result in a technical foul and a point awarded against the offender.

4.J.2.   If the server serves the ball while the receiver is signaling "not ready," the ball will be re-served with no penalty and the server shall be "warned" by the referee to check the receiver. If the server continues to serve without checking the receiver, the referee may call a technical foul and award a point to the receiver's score.

4.J.3.   After the score is called, if the server looks at the receiver and the receiver is not signaling "not ready," the server may then serve. If the receiver attempts to signal "not ready" after the serve is made, then the serve stands, whether or not the ball is returned.

USAPA Comment: A receiver who attempts to return the service shall be considered to have been ready. If the receiver has signaled not ready, the service must be replayed.

Section 5: Service Sequence Rules (Revised 5/1/07)

5.A. Singles.

5.A.1. At the start of each game, the server begins the serve on the right side and alternates from right to left to right, etc., as long as the server holds serve.

5.A.2. The server must serve to the crosscourt (court diagonally opposite) service court.

5.A.3. The server's score will always be even (0, 2, 4, 6, 8, 10...) when serving from the right side and odd (1, 3, 5, 7, 9...) when serving from the left side (only in singles play).

5.B. Doubles.

5.B.1. The service always starts in the right-hand court and alternates from right to left to right, etc., as long as server holds serve.

5.B.2. The server must serve to the crosscourt (court diagonally opposite) service court. There is no restriction on the position of the server's partner.

5.B.3. The team's points will be even when the starting server is on the right-hand side. Points will be odd when the starting server is on the left-hand side.

5.B.4. The team serving the initial serve of a game can commit only one fault before service is passed on to the opposing team. After that, each team member serves until that player loses the serve when the team commits a fault. After both players have lost their serves, the serve passes to the opposing team.

5.B.5. The server will alternate between right and left service courts upon scoring a point. After the first server's team faults, the second server will continue to serve from that server's last side position and then alternate positions as long as the serving team continues to win points.

5.B.6. If the ball is served by the wrong team member or from the wrong court, the service is a fault. If the fault was by the first server, then the first service is lost and the correct second server serves from the correct service position. If the fault was by the second server, then it is a side out. A point made from an incorrect service position or an incorrect server will not be retained unless play has continued and another point has been scored or the opposing team has served.

5.B.7. The receiver is the person on the diagonally opposite side of the court from the server. In doubles, this position corresponds to the player's score and starting position.

5.B.8. The receiver is the only player who may return the ball. If the wrong player returns the ball, it is a point for the serving team.

5.B.9. The receiver's partner may stand anywhere on or off the court.

5.B.10. The receiving team does not alternate positions when a point is scored by the serving team. The receiving team may switch positions after the return of serve, but after the rally is over, the players must return back to their original positions, which correspond to the team's score and the players' starting positions.

USAPA Comments:

- When an incorrect serve is recognized immediately after the rally, the point does not count.

- When an incorrect serve is not recognized until the server has lost the serve, the most recent point scored by that server on an illegal serve, if any, does not count.

- When an incorrect serve is not recognized until the server has lost the serve and the partner has scored a point on the serve, the point of the first server counts. If the point scored by the partner is also the result of an illegal serve, that point does not count.

- When an incorrect serve is not recognized until after the opposing team has served, points scored on the previous serves count.

5.C. **Service/Side Selection and Rotation.**

5.C.1.　A coin flip or any other fair method will determine first choice of service or side. If the winner chooses to serve or receive, the loser picks starting side. If the winner chooses starting side, the loser chooses to serve or receive.

5.C.2.　Sides and initial service will be switched upon completion of each game.

5.C.3.　Sides will be switched in a third game (if the match is 2 out of 3 games) after the first team reaches a score of 6 points. Serve remains with the player holding serve.

5.C.4.　In games to 15, sides will be switched after the first team reaches a score of 8 points. Serve remains with the player holding serve.

5.C.5.　In games to 21, sides will be switched after the first team reaches a score of 11 points. Serve remains with the player holding serve.

Section 6: Line Call Rules (Revised 5/1/07)

6.A. Served balls that clear the non-volley line and land on any other service court line are good.

6.B. Balls in play (except on serve, see 6.A) that land on any court line are good.

6.C. A ball contacting the floor outside of the baseline or sideline, even though the edge of the ball overlaps the line, is considered out of bounds.

6.D. Code of Ethics for Line-Calling. Pickleball is played according to specific rules. It also requires a code of ethics for line-calling responsibilities when performed by players.

The line-calling responsibilities of players are different from those assigned to referees or lines people. The officials make impartial judgment calls with all players' interests in mind. The player, when assigned line-calling duties, operates under the principle that all questionable calls must be resolved in favor of the opponent.

The basic elements are:

6.D.1. Players will call the lines on their side of the court (excluding the non-volley line, if being called by a referee).

6.D.2. The opponent gets the benefit of the doubt on line calls made.

6.D.3. Spectators should not be consulted on any line calls. Spectators may be prejudiced, unqualified, or not in position to see the call, and therefore cannot participate.

6.D.4. All participants should strive for accuracy in making line calls.

6.D.5. No player should question an opponent's call unless asked (except that any player may appeal a call to the referee in an officiated match). A player should ask the opponent's opinion if the opponent was in a better position to see the call. An opponent's opinion, if requested, should be accepted. The opinion of a player looking down the line is more likely to be accurate than one looking across the line.

6.D.6. Don't call a ball "out" when you are looking across the line unless you can clearly see the space between the line and the ball as it hits. The player's depth of field judgment, based on the laws of parallax, prevent accurate judgment in these cases.

6.D.7. All "let" or "out" calls must be made "instantly"; otherwise the ball is presumed good and still in play. "Instantly" is defined as calling "let" or "out" prior to the ball being hit by the opponent or before it has gone out of play.

6.D.8. Any ball that cannot be called "out" is presumed to be "in." The player cannot claim a "let" (replay) because the ball was not seen. The opponent's opinion can be requested, and, if the opponent says the ball was "in" or the opponent could not see it, the ball must be declared "in."

6.D.9. Players should not request a "let" (replay) because they were not sure the ball was "out" or "in." In this case, benefit of the doubt goes to the opponent.

6.D.10. In doubles play, if one player calls the ball "out" and the partner calls it "in," then doubt exists, and the ball must be declared "in" (except that any player may appeal a call to the referee in an officiated match).

6.D.11. Line calls should be promptly signaled by hand or voice, regardless of how obvious they may seem.

6.D.12. If, while the ball is in the air, a player yells "out," "no," "bounce it," or any other word to communicate to his or her partner that the ball may be out, it shall be considered player communication. If the ball lands in, play will continue. If the out call is made after the ball has hit the court surface, it shall be considered a line call and play shall stop.

Section 7: Fault Rules (Revised 11/01/07)

A fault is any action that stops play or creates a violation of the rules. A fault will be declared for the following:

7.A. Hitting the ball into the net on the service or any return.

7.B. Hitting the ball out of bounds.

7.C. Failure to hit the ball before it bounces twice on the player's court.

7.D. Violation of a service rule (See Section 4).

7.E. A player, player's clothing, or any part of a player's paddle touches the net or the net post when the ball is in play.

7.F. The ball in play strikes a player or anything the player is wearing or carrying. There is one exception to this rule: if the ball strikes the player's paddle hand below the wrist, the ball is still in play. If the ball strikes a player standing out of bounds, that player loses the rally. In doubles, if the serve strikes the receiver's partner, it is a point for the serving team, providing it is not a let serve. This rule also includes balls that appear to be hit out of bounds: during play, if you catch the ball or try to stop it from heading out of bounds, you lose the rally.

USAPA Comment: If the player is in the process of changing hands with both hands on the paddle, or is attempting a two-handed stroke and either hand is hit below the wrist, then the ball is considered in play.

7.G. A ball in play strikes any permanent object before bouncing on the court.

USAPA Comment: If the ball in play hits a permanent object after it has bounced on the court, the player who hit the ball wins the point. If the ball in play hits a permanent object before it bounces on the court, the player who hit the ball loses the point.

7.H. Violation of non-volley zone rules (See Section 9).

7.I. Violation of the other rules (See Section 12).

7.J. The serve is made by bouncing the ball off the court surface before hitting it.

7.K. A player hits the ball before it passes the plane of the net.

Section 8:   Dead Ball Rules (Revised 11/01/07)

8.A.   A dead ball is declared after any action that stops play.

8.B.   A ball is not declared dead until it has bounced twice or has violated one of the fault rules (See Section 7).

8.C.   A hinder called by the referee or player will result in a dead ball and a replay.

Section 9:   Non-Volley Zone Rules (Revised 11/01/07)

9.A.   The non-volley zone is the area of the court bounded by the two sidelines, the non-volley line, and the net. The non-volley line and the sidelines are included in the non-volley zone.

9.B.   A fault will be declared if, in the act of volleying the ball, a player or anything the player is wearing or carrying touches the non-volley zone or touches any non-volley line. For example, a fault will be declared if, in the act of volleying the ball, one of the player's feet touches a non-volley line.

9.C.   A fault will be declared if, in the act of volleying the ball, the player's momentum causes the player or anything the player is wearing or carrying to touch the non-volley zone or touch any non-volley line. It is a fault even if the ball is declared dead before the player touches the non-volley zone.

9.D.   A fault will be declared if the player violates the intent of the non-volley zone rule. All volleys must be initiated outside of the non-volley zone. A maneuver such as standing within the non-volley zone, jumping up to hit a volley, and then landing outside the non-volley zone is prohibited. If a player is inside the non-volley zone for any reason, that player cannot volley the return until both feet are on the court surface outside the non-volley zone.

9.E.   A player may step on the non-volley line or enter the non-volley zone at any time except when that player is volleying the ball. There is no violation if your partner returns the ball while you are standing in the non-volley zone. A player may enter the non-volley zone before or after returning any ball that bounces.

9.F. A player may stay inside the non-volley zone to return balls that bounce. That is, there is no violation if a player does not exit the non-volley zone after hitting a ball that bounces.

Section 10: Scoring - Game - Match Rules
(Revised 11/01/07)

10.A. **Scoring.** Only the serving team can score points.

10.B. Points are scored by legally serving a ball that is not touched by the opponent (an ace) or by winning the rally (faulting by the opponent).

10.C. **Game.** The first side scoring 11 points and leading by at least a 2-point margin wins. If both sides are tied at 10 points, then play continues until one side wins by 2 points.

10.D. **Standard Tournament Format.** Best 2 of 3 games to 11 points.

10.E. **Alternate Tournament Format.** A tournament director may choose to have some or all matches consist of one game to 15 points or one game to 21 points with a win by 2 points. A winning margin of one point would be appropriate for round robin events where the winners are determined by the total number of points rather than the most number of matches won.

Section 11: Time-Out Rules (Revised 11/01/07)

11.A. **Normal Time-Outs.** A player or team is entitled to 2 time-outs per game; each time-out period shall last only 1 minute. Then play must be resumed or another time-out must be called by either side. Time-outs may never be called once the ball is in play or the server has started the serving motion. For games to 21 points, each team is allowed 3 time-outs per game.

11.B. **Injury Time-Outs.** If a player is injured during a match, that player may call an injury time-out. The referee must agree that an injury did take place and that the player is not just stalling to rest or recuperate. If the referee agrees, then that player will be allowed no more than 15 minutes of rest during the injury time-out. If the player cannot resume play after the 15-minute injury time-out period, the match shall be awarded to the opponents.

11.C. **Equipment Time-Outs.** Players are expected to keep all clothing and equipment in good playable condition and are expected to use regular time-outs and time between games for adjustments and replacement of equipment. If a player or team is out of time-outs and the referee determines that an equipment change or adjustment is necessary for fair and safe continuation of the match, the referee may award an equipment time-out not to exceed 2 minutes.

11.D. **Between Games Time-Out.** Between games time-outs shall not exceed 2 minutes between each game of a match.

11.E. **Postponed Games.** Any game postponed by referees shall be resumed with the same score and remaining time-outs as when postponed.

USAPA Comment: When a time-out is called, the referee may request that all players place their paddles on the correct court and the ball be placed under the serving player's paddle.

Section 12: Other Rules (Revised 5/01/08)

12.A. **Carry and Double Hits.** Balls hit during one continuous single-direction stroke are legal, even though they may be unintentionally hit twice or "carried." Only when there is a definite second push by the player does the shot become illegal.

12.B. **Switching Hands.** A paddle may be switched from hand to hand at any time. Two-handed shots are also legal.

12.C. **Return Attempts.** A completely missed return shot does not, by itself, constitute a dead ball. The ball remains in play until it bounces twice or until any other fault has occurred.

12.D. **Broken or Cracked Ball.** Play continues until the end of the rally. If, in the judgment of the referee, a broken or cracked ball affected the outcome of the rally, the referee shall call for a replay.

12.E. **Injury During Game.** Rally continues to its conclusion, despite an injury to any of the players.

12.F. **Player Equipment Problem.** A rally shall not be stopped or affected if a player loses or breaks a paddle or loses a personal item.

12.G. **Items on the Court.** If anything a player is wearing or carrying lands on the court, it becomes part of the court. Therefore, if a ball in play hits the item on the court, the ball remains in play. If the item lands on the opponent's court, it is a fault. If the item lands in the non-volley zone as a result of a volley, it is a fault.

12.H. **Distractions.** Players may not yell, stamp their feet, or otherwise try to distract an opponent when the opponent is about to play the ball. In Doubles, team communication shall not normally be considered a distraction. However, loud communication at the time the opponent is about to strike the ball may be considered a distraction. If, in the judgment of the referee, a distraction has occurred, it shall result in the loss of the rally.

12.I. **The Net Posts.** The net posts are positioned out of bounds. If a ball strikes the net post or anything attached to the net post, it is a fault and a dead ball is declared. This rule does not include the net, the net cable, or rope between the net posts.

12.J. The Net.

    12.J.1. The net and the wires or strings holding up the net are positioned (mostly) on the court. Therefore, if the ball strikes the top of the net or strikes the top net wire or string and lands in bounds, then it remains in play.

    12.J.2. Hitting the ball between the top and bottom net wires is a fault.

    12.J.3. If the ball bounces into a player's non-volley zone with enough backspin as to cause it to return back over the net, that player may reach over the net to hit the ball but may not touch the net. The player is also allowed to go around the net post and cross the imaginary extension of the net so long as he or she does not touch the opponent's court.

    12.J.4. If a player hits the ball over the net into the opponent's court, and then the ball bounces back over the net without being touched by the opponent, the striking player wins the rally.

12.K. Shots Around the Net Post. If a ball hit at an angle bounces in the court and travels beyond the sidelines, a player may return the ball around the outside of the net post. The ball does not need to travel back over the net. In addition, there is no restriction on the height of the return. For example, a player may return the ball around the net post below the height of the net.

12.L. Coaching. Players may consult with coaches or any other person during time-outs and between games. Coaching of players between points is allowed as long as it is not disruptive, does not delay the game, and consists only of instructions to the player, not a conversation between the coach and player. A conversation between a player and any person performing a coaching function shall result in a time-out charged to the player or team. If the team is out of time-outs, then the conversation may result in a technical warning or technical foul. Coaching is not allowed between the time that the referee calls the score and the end of the rally.

Section 13: Sanctioned Tournament Formats
(Revised 5/01/08)

13.A. **Tournament Formats.**

There are five tournament formats that may be used. The particular format is typically the choice of the Tournament Sponsor or the Tournament Director.

13.A.1. **Single Elimination with Consolation.** The loser is out of the winner's bracket. First-round losers go into a consolation bracket.

13.A.2. **Double Elimination.** A loss will put the loser into a lower bracket. The winner of the lower bracket will play the winner of the top bracket for the championship. If the winner of the lower bracket wins, then a tie-breaker match must be played.

13.A.3. **Drop Flight.** All players start at the top level. First-round losers will drop into the second level. First-round losers of the second level will drop into the third level and so on. The winner of a first-round match in any level stays at that level. There may be a lower bracket for the second-round losers of each level.

13.A.4. **Round Robin.** All players will play each other. The player or team winning the most matches is declared the winner. Alternatively, the player or team winning the most points may be declared the winner.

13.A.5. **Point Award.** Similar to a Round Robin, but 1 point is awarded for each win. No points are awarded for a loss. In addition, a player or team winning the match by winning the first 2 games receives an additional point.

13.B. **Draws.**

13.B.1. If possible, all draws shall be made at least 2 days before the tournament commences.

13.B.2. The Draw and Seeding Committee shall be appointed by the Tournament Director.

13.C. **Notice of Matches.** It is the responsibility of each player to check the posted schedules to determine the time and place of each match. If any change is made in the schedule after posting, the Tournament Director or his designated representative shall notify the players of the change.

13.D. **Forfeited Matches.** A forfeit is a loss by default. It usually occurs because a player or team did not show up on time, because of player injury, or for misconduct. A player or team forfeiting a match for any reason shall lose the match as if that player or team lost all games of that match. Therefore, the other player or team wins the match as if that player or team won all games of that match. The winning player or team shall receive the appropriate point score or advance to the next level.

13.E. **Lower Bracket Matches.** In all USAPA-sanctioned tournaments, each entrant shall be entitled to participate in a minimum of two scheduled matches per event entered. This means that losers of their first match shall have the opportunity to compete in the event's lower bracket. The lower bracket matches may be modified at the discretion of the Tournament Director (e.g., one game to 15 points), but this modification must be announced either verbally or in writing to all players before the tournament begins or on the tournament application. If a first match is scheduled with an opponent who must "forfeit for any reason," then that scheduled match is considered a "win." The Tournament Director is not at fault if a player or team wins their first match by forfeit and then loses a second match and thus only plays one match. This is known as "luck of the draw," and the player or team falling into this category will not go into lower bracket play.

13.F. **Scheduling Matches.** If one or more contestants are entered in multiple events, they may be required to play multiple events on the same day or night with little rest between matches. This is a risk assumed on entering multiple events. If possible, the schedule should provide a rest period between matches.

13.G. **Doubles Play.** A Doubles team shall consist of 2 players who meet the classification requirements to participate in a particular division of play. In an event based upon rating, the higher-rated player determines the team's ability level (or division or classification). In an adult (19 & over) event based upon age grouping, the lowest age of one of the team members will determine the team's classification. Players may play down in a younger division unless prohibited by the rules of the National Senior Games Association. Juniors (18 & under) may enter any Junior age-division event for which they are not too old as well as the adult division of 19 & over. Under no circumstances can a partner change be made after the partners have begun team play. A partner change may be made prior to the first-round match if, in the opinion of the tournament director, the change is due to injury, illness, or circumstances beyond the control of the player.

13.H. **Court Changes.** In USAPA-sanctioned tournaments, the Tournament Director may decide on a change of courts after the completion of any tournament game if such a change will accommodate better spectator or playing conditions.

13.I. **Tournament Conduct.** In USAPA-sanctioned tournaments, the referee is empowered to call technical fouls and to forfeit a match if an individual player's behavior is detrimental to the tournament. In addition, the Tournament Director has the authority to expel any player for misconduct, no matter how many technical fouls have been received.

Section 14: Tournament Management and Officiating
(Revised 11/01/07)

14.A. **Tournament Director.** A Tournament Director shall manage the tournament. It is the Tournament Director's responsibility to designate the officials and their areas of responsibility.

14.B. **Rules Briefing.** Before the tournament, all officials and players shall be briefed or supplied with the current rules about court hinders. This briefing should be put in writing when possible. The current USAPA tournament rules will apply and be made available. The Tournament Director may not impose any local rule or use any interpretation of any rule not stated within the current USAPA rules. Any exception to the rules that is desired because of physical limitations of the court or other local conditions must be approved in advance by the USAPA.

14.C. **Officials.** Every USAPA-sanctioned tournament must have a referee for each match. The Tournament Director or the Tournament Director's representative will assign all referees. Although any tournament player may volunteer to referee a match, the Tournament Director or designated representative will have the final say on referee assignments. Officials may also include lines people at the discretion of the Tournament Director.

14.D. **Referee's Duties.**

Before each match begins, the referee must:

14.D.1. Check on preparation of court with respect to cleanliness, lighting, height of the net, court markings, and haz-ards.

14.D.2. Check on availability and suitability of necessary materi-als for the match such as balls, score cards, pen-cils, and location of the clock.

14.D.3. Check to ensure that planned support is available (i.e., lines people, scorekeeper, etc.).

14.D.4. Meet with players at courtside to:

14.D.4.a. Inspect paddles for irregularities.

14.D.4.b. Instruct players on the need to wait for the referee to call out the score before serving.

14.D.4.c. Point out court hindrances and other approved rule modifications.

14.D.4.d. Instruct players on line-calling duties of referee, lines people, and players.

14.D.4.e. Use any fair method to determine initial service and side.

During the match, the referee must:

14.D.5. Re-check the net height if the net is disturbed.

14.D.6. Call the score after each point is played and that point has been marked down on the official scorecard. Calling out the score indicates to each side that play is ready to resume.

14.E. **Line Calls.**

Accepted hand signals are:

- Line faults - outstretched arm pointing in direction of the out-of-bounds ball path.

- Fair ball - arms extended parallel to court with palms down.

14.E.1. **Officiating Options.**

14.E.1.a. Players call all lines (generally used in non-tournament play).

14.E.1.b. The referee calls non-volley zone infractions. Players make their own calls on other lines on their side of court (generally used in tournaments).

14.E.1.c. The referee calls non-volley zone infractions. Lines people make calls for sidelines and baselines (generally restricted to tournament medal matches).

14.E.2. **Lines People.**

14.E.2.a. It is recommended that lines people be assigned to medal matches. The Tournament

Director or designated representative will select lines people.

14.E2.b. Lines people will call all line faults within their jurisdiction and will signify fault by calling "out."

14.F. **Referee's Officiating Duties.** The referee is responsible for all decisions related to procedural and judgment calls during the match. If the players make the line calls and there is a disputed line call, the players may request that the referee determine the line call. The referee's call will stand. If the referee cannot make the line call, the player's call stands. Spectators are not part of the game and, therefore, cannot be consulted on calls.

14.G. In doubles, if players on the same side disagree on a line call made by one of them on their side of the court, one of the players may ask the referee for a ruling. If the referee clearly saw the play, the referee shall make a ruling based on observation. If the referee cannot make the call, the ball is good.

14.H. **Match Forfeiture.**

14.H.1. A referee may impose a forfeit when a player refuses to abide by the referee's decision or engages in unsports- manlike conduct.

14.H.2. A referee may impose a forfeit for failure to comply with the tournament or host facility's rules while on the premises, or for improper conduct on the premises between matches, or for abuse of hospitality, locker room, or other rules and procedures.

14.H.3. A referee may impose a forfeit when a player fails to report to play 10 minutes after the match has been called to play. The Tournament Director may permit a longer delay if circumstances warrant such a decision.

14.H.4. A player receiving 2 technical fouls in a match shall auto- matically forfeit that match. In addition, the Tournament Director has the authority to expel any player from the tournament for misconduct.

14.I. **Appeals.** Appeals to the referee regarding judgment calls (line calls, double bounce, etc.) will be decided by the referee. The referee may consult players or lines people to decide the outcome of the appeal.

    14.I.1.   A player may appeal a procedural or judgment call to the referee. The referee will consider procedural appeals and will provide a decision.

    14.I.2.   A referee's decision will either result in a point awarded, a service loss, or a replay.

    14.I.3.   A player wishing to signify an appeal during a rally may do so by raising his or her non-paddle hand to inform the referee that an appeal is being made regarding a previous possible violation. Play will continue until the rally is over and appeal can then be made.

    14.I.4.   Replays. After reviewing an appeal, the referee may determine that no decision on the appeal can be made and may direct a replay.

14.J. **Rules Interpretations.** If a player feels that the referee has interpreted the rules incorrectly, that player may request that the referee or the Tournament Director show the applicable rule in the rulebook.

14.K. **Protest.** Any referee's decision involving an interpretation of the rules may, on protest, be decided by the Tournament Director.

14.L. **Removal of a Referee or Lines Person.** A referee or lines person may be removed when both players in singles or both teams in doubles agree to the removal or at the discretion of the Tournament Director. In the event that the removal of a referee or lines person is requested by only one player or team and not agreed to by the other player or team, then the Tournament Director may accept or reject the request. If a referee or lines person is removed, the Tournament Director will appoint the new referee or lines person.

14.M.**Technical Fouls.** The referee is empowered to call technical fouls. When a technical foul is called, 1 point shall be added to the score of the opposing side. After the technical foul is called, if the play is not immediately continued, or the player continues to be abusive, then the referee is empowered to forfeit the match in favor of the opponents. If a player or a team receives 2 technical fouls in a match, then that match shall automatically result in forfeiture. In addition, the Tournament Director has the authority to expel any player or team from the tournament for misconduct. If a player has been expelled from a tournament, any prizes and ranking points gained from the tournament shall not be forfeited.

Actions that may result in technical fouls are:

14.M.1. A player using objectionable or demeaning language directed at another person shall incur a technical warning or a technical foul, depending upon its severity. Once a technical warning has been issued, the second offense will result in a technical foul. Excessive profanity used for any reason shall incur similar action. The referee will determine the severity of any violation.

14.M.2. Excessive arguing.

14.M.3. Threats of any nature to any person.

14.M.4. Purposely breaking the ball or striking of the ball between rallies.

14.M.5. Intentionally throwing the paddle. If this action results in the striking or injury of any person or damage to the court or facility, an automatic technical foul shall be assessed against the offender and a point shall be awarded to the opponent.

14.M.6. Delay of game, either in the form of taking too much time during time-outs or between games, in excessive questioning of the referee on the rules, or in excessive or unnecessary appeals.

14.M.7. Any other actions that are considered unsportsmanlike behavior.

14.N. **Technical Warning.** If a player's behavior is not severe enough to warrant a technical foul, a technical warning may be issued. In most situations, the referee should give a technical warning before imposing a technical foul. Points shall not be awarded for a technical warning.

14.O. **Effect of Technical Fouls and Technical Warnings.** A technical warning shall not result in a loss of rally or point awarded and shall be accompanied by a brief explanation of the reason for the warning. If a referee issues a technical foul, 1 point shall be added to the non-offender's score. A called technical foul or warning shall have no effect on service change or side out. If a point is awarded, the player or team awarded the point must change positions to reflect the score after the awarding of the point.

Section 15: Sanctioned Tournament Division Categories (Revised 1/14/08)

15.A. **Event Categories.**

- Men - Singles and Doubles

- Women - Singles and Doubles

- Mixed - Doubles

    15.A.1. In events described by gender, only members of that gender shall be allowed to play in that event.

    15.A.2. Mixed Doubles - A mixed doubles team shall consist of 1 male and 1 female player.

15.B. **List of USAPA-Approved Events.** The list of approved events is in the rankings document on the USAPA website.

15.C. **Guidelines for Moving Between Ability-Level Divisions.** Guidelines for moving between ability-level divisions are addressed in the ratings document on the USAPA website.

Index

A

Aerobics 68
    endurance 71
Angle
    paddle 15, 20, 21, 22, 23

B

Backhand
    grip 19
    groundstroke 33
      problems 35
    serve 39
      problems 39
Backspin 57
Ball 9
    Cosom 9
    Dura 9
    Jugs 9
    Pickle-Ball, Inc. 9
    Singapore 9
    when to hit it 26
Body positions 15, 24
    bending your knees 24
    hitting a smash 28
    hitting a volley 27
    hitting the ball after a
      bounce 26
    when to hit the ball 26
Bounce
    hitting the ball 26

C

Closed face 23
Clothing 12
Converting tennis courts 13
Court 11
    dimensions 11
    playing surface 11
Court position 59
    during a serve 61
    moving into position 63
    non-volley zone 59
    serve 61, 62
    shuffle 63
    strongest 59
    weakest 59

D

Dink 52
    problems 53
Double bounce rule 2
Doubles 110
    serving position 62
Drop shot 49
    problems 50
Drop volley 49
    problems 50
Dynamic stretching 69

T

Tennis court conversion 13
Topspin 57

U

Underspin 57
USAPA (United States of
     America Pickleball Associ-
     ation) 1

V

Volley 2, 41
     hitting the ball 27
     problems 43

W

Warm-ups 67
     stretching 67
When to hit the ball 26
     after a bounce 26
     smash 28
     volley 27

The Art of Pickleball won the Arizona Book Award
for Recreation/Sports in 2007.

Gale H. Leach lives in Arizona
with her husband and three cats.